Changing Faces, Changing Places

Mapping Southern Californians

James P. Allen and Eugene Turner

The Center for Geographical Studies · California State University, Northridge

The Center for Geographical Studies
Department of Geography
California State University, Northridge
Northridge, California 91330-8249
Copyright ©2002 by The Center for Geographical Studies
All rights reserved. Published 2002

ISBN 0-9656966-2-6 (pbk.)

Library of Congress Cataloging-in-Publication Data

Allen, James Paul, 1936-
  Changing faces, changing places : mapping Southern Californians /
James P. Allen and Eugene Turner.
      p. cm.
Includes bibliographical references.
  ISBN 0-9656966-2-6 (pbk. : alk. paper)
  1. Ethnology--California, Southern. 2. Ethnology--California,
Southern--Maps. 3. Ethnology--California, Southern--Statistics. 4.
California, Southern--Population--Maps. 5. California,
Southern--Population--Statistics. I. Turner, Eugene, 1946- II. Title.
  F867 .A445 2002
  304.6'09794'9--dc21
                                    2002011123

Printed in the United States of America

The paper used in this publication meets the minimum requirements of the
American National Standard for Information Sciences—Permanence of Paper
for Printed Library Materials, ANSI Z39.48-1992.

Contents

Illustrations

Photo Credits: Maria D. Ivey, pages 14, 16, 24, 27, 31, 33, 37, 40, 41, 46, 48, 51
Eugene Turner, pages 39, 44, 52

Tables

1. Introduction

Any person who lived in Southern California before 1960 but moved away for forty years might have difficulty recognizing parts of it today. In that time the population has more than doubled. Land between towns that was once empty or farmed is now occupied so that many places appear to have merged, and old downtowns of many cities have been rebuilt or remodeled. On the metropolitan fringe, shopping centers and gated tracts of new homes now replace open country. All the cities, suburbs, and small towns have become better interconnected by phones, fax machines, freeways, and commuter trains. Southern California has also seen a major loss of older heavy industry (steel, automobiles, tires, etc.) and an increase in apparel manufacturing, high-tech development facilities, large retail stores, and new office buildings. Less evident would be the underlying employment shifts that reflect urban economic restructuring.[1]

What may be the most striking change of all is the people. Since the late 1960s immigrants and their children have reshaped the region's demographic composition, have simulated its economy and politics, and have adapted culturally and economically. The population that was once overwhelmingly White, with roots in the Midwestern and Eastern United States, now looks very different and captures the diversity of peoples on this planet.

Purpose of the Book

This book takes the changes observed in the ethnic make-up of Southern Californians and shows how these have played out in different places. We do this by mapping and interpreting ethnic group distributions as of 2000 and changes that occurred during the 1990s. In our concern with tying down general processes to specific places, we are acting very much as geographers. The perspective of geography emphasizes places—the meaning of their relative locations, their changing character and its significance, and the interconnections that weave them together as a functioning region and as a broad spatial pattern.

Changing Faces, Changing Places, then, becomes a window on the continuing evolution of the different peoples and places in urban Southern California. It builds upon our earlier volume, *The Ethnic Quilt: Population Diversity in Southern California*.[2] However, the present book tells a different story, one focusing more on recent ethnic changes in the cities and suburbs of the massive Los Angeles metropolitan area. Its maps make use of Census 2000 data to portray the most up-to-date distributions of ethnic groups that are possible. Even more useful are this book's maps of ethnic change in neighborhoods during the nineties. No such change maps were included in *The Ethnic Quilt*. Nearly all references cited in *Changing Faces, Changing Places* are different from and more recent than those used for *The Ethnic Quilt*. We hope students, scholars, and other researchers will find such recently available sources of value. On the other hand, *The Ethnic Quilt* remains the more complete source for historical details of ethnic neighborhood settlements, for comparative analyses of the socioeconomic characteristics of ethnic populations, and for explanations of immigration since 1970.

Apart from understanding recent change in Southern California for its own sake, we expect that many of our findings are applicable in a general way to other large metropolitan areas in the United States. The urban changes occurring here also characterize many other metropolitan areas, but the very large absolute numbers of Latinos and Asians in our region are exceptional. Such large populations may make incipient trends and patterns more visible or evident here than in other metropolitan areas where those numbers are smaller. This means also that what has been happening here regarding ethnic relations and patterns is likely to happen elsewhere. Thus, the patterns and findings of this book and other research on Southern California may provide glimpses into the future of metropolitan America.[3]

The Los Angeles Metropolitan Area

An interconnected area. Nearly half of all the 34 million people in California live in the area treated in this book—a five-county area including and surrounding Los Angeles. The five counties of Los Angeles, Orange, Riverside, San Bernardino, and Ventura are collectively a single massive metropolitan area, technically named by federal officials the Los Angeles-Riverside-Orange County Consolidated Metropolitan Statistical Area (CMSA). We often refer to this same area as "Southern California," "the Los Angeles metropolitan area," or "the Los Angeles CMSA."

The oldest and largest component of the five-county region is Los Angeles County, within which lies the city of the same name, the second largest city in the United States. The four outlying counties represent essentially the outer suburbs of Los Angeles County.

Suburbanization (or spatial decentralization) around Los Angeles and other older towns and cities has been taking place for over a century. Many of these formerly independent places have grown together so that little vacant land remains between them. These same decentralizing and coalescing processes have been occurring around nearly all other medium-sized and large American cities, though often not to the degree found in Southern California. Altogether, the population of the five-county Los Angeles area grew by 12 percent during the 1990s, slightly faster than the 11-percent average for the nine U.S. metropolitan areas of over five million.

People have typically moved to the suburbs to escape problems of cities such as higher crime, to find newer and cheaper single-family houses and better schools, and, in some cases, to avoid increasing numbers of poorer or different people in their neighborhoods. Most have been pleased with life in the suburbs. Residents of Orange and Ventura Counties are, on average, more satisfied with their localities than people who live in older suburbs like the San Fernando Valley or the older portions of Los Angeles City.[4] On the other hand, those who move to more distant places like Palmdale and Victorville in the Mojave Desert or Temecula and Moreno Valley in Riverside County must often put up with very long daily commutes to work in return for the lower housing prices in those outer areas.

Although most residents of the four surrounding counties probably do not think of themselves as part of this massive metropolitan area, they are in many ways tied together with Los Angeles County. Concerts, sports events, other types of entertainment and recreation, and jobs draw people from all over the region. Major television and print-media organizations cover events across Southern California, and people visit friends and relatives on other sides of the region. Numerous businesses have branch offices in different counties but often use firms in Los Angeles County for business and professional services such as auditors, attorneys, and investment banking. All this is recognized by the federal government and by the many scholars who treat these five counties together as we do—as a single metropolitan area.[5]

Such interconnections among the five counties can be illustrated by patterns of commuting. Although these data are based on 1990, the patterns have probably changed little (Figure 1.1). The daily flows between Los Angeles and Orange Counties are exceptionally large in both directions. Over one hundred fifty thousand people make a daily trip from homes in Riverside and San Bernardino Counties to jobs in Los Angeles County, and half that number come in from Ventura County.

Comparing L. A. to other metropolitan areas. Until about thirty years ago most people writing about Los Angeles viewed it as an exceptional place, where the people and their attitudes and behaviors were different from those in other parts of the country. However, the growth of various social science disciplines, including urban geography, has prompted more comparative quantitative analysis of the characteristics of different places. The net effect has been to show that Los Angeles is not really so exceptional as was once thought. It is one of many large metropolitan areas. Whether the topic is commuting time to work, occupational structure, income growth rates, or suburban job growth, research findings do not usually show it to be an extreme case. Thus, where appropriate, we compare L.A. to other metropolitan areas, as we do frequently in our section on ethnic residential separation in chapter 7.

In its urban development over the last thirty years Los Angeles illustrates widespread patterns and processes.[6] As journalist Joel Garreau observed, "Every single American city that *is* growing, is growing in the fashion of Los Angeles, with multiple urban cores."[7] Over the country the dispersal of houses, industry, shopping centers, and office buildings into the adjacent countryside has resulted in massive sprawl extending far beyond older built-up areas. Population and employment decentralization have characterized nearly all large metropolitan areas in the United States.[8]

To illustrate locally, 71 percent of all the people in the five-county region lived in Los Angeles County in 1970, but by 2000 the comparable figure had dropped to 58 percent. The percentage of all the region's private-sector employment that was located in Los Angeles County dropped from 76 percent in 1972 to 64 percent in 1992.[9] Comparing rates of population and employment concentration in the Los Angeles CMSA demonstrates that residences are slightly more suburbanized than employment. However, the difference is not large and jobs may be deconcentrating more rapidly than people. Although differences in job-population proportions demonstrate the need for commuting into Los Angeles County, each county has an intricate and changing mix of housing areas and employment of different types.

Because new focuses of business and employment in "edge cities" have often appeared in outlying areas, today's metropolitan areas are often thought of as multi-centered or polycentric.[10] There are perhaps two dozen edge cities in Southern California including Century City, the Los Angeles Airport (LAX) area, Pasadena, Glendale, Warner Center in the San Fernando Valley, Irvine Spectrum in Orange County, and Ontario Center in San Bernardino County.[11] Certainly, the old notion of a single downtown or business center in a central city surrounded by its suburbs is out of date for Los Angeles and almost all other large metropolitan areas.

Our Approach

Interpretation of ethnic patterns. We interpret the mapped patterns in terms of various processes of economic and cultural change, population concentration and deconcentration, and ethnic group interrelations as these have been studied in geography, history, and the social sciences. An important characteristic of people is their socioeconomic status or social class. Ethnic groups differ greatly in average status with respect to educational attainment, occupation, and income. Thus, both social status and ethnic identity are keys to understanding residential locations of individuals and groups.

One recurring theme in *Changing Faces, Changing Places* concerns the relative residential concentration or dispersal of ethnic groups. The leading theoretical explanation of such patterns relates the cultural and economic assimilation of ethnic groups to their spatial assimilation. In essence, people with better English-language skills, education, and greater familiarity with the dominant culture (more assimilated culturally) are more likely to work in occupations that provide higher incomes (more assimilated economically), and people with these two characteristics tend to choose to move outside ethnic neighborhoods (more assimilated spatially). Familiarity with research on these matters led to our measurement of changing ethnic enclaves and guided other aspects of our interpretation.[12]

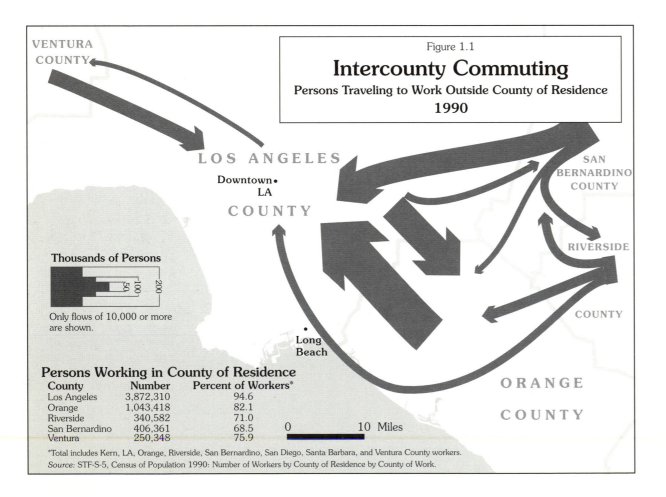

Figure 1.1

Intercounty Commuting
Persons Traveling to Work Outside County of Residence
1990

VENTURA COUNTY

LOS ANGELES COUNTY

Downtown LA

SAN BERNARDINO COUNTY

RIVERSIDE COUNTY

Long Beach

ORANGE COUNTY

Thousands of Persons

200
100
50

Only flows of 10,000 or more are shown.

0　　10 Miles

Persons Working in County of Residence

County	Number	Percent of Workers*
Los Angeles	3,872,310	94.6
Orange	1,043,418	82.1
Riverside	340,582	71.0
San Bernardino	406,361	68.5
Ventura	250,348	75.9

*Total includes Kern, LA, Orange, Riverside, San Bernardino, San Diego, Santa Barbara, and Ventura County workers.
Source: STF-S-5, Census of Population 1990: Number of Workers by County of Residence by County of Work.

Areal coverage in maps and tables. In this book we portray the latest ethnic distributions and recent changes for the largest portion of urban and suburban Southern California. Because most of the newer suburban neighborhoods are located in those outlying counties, we wanted our maps to cover the most important parts of those counties.

Los Angeles and Orange Counties have complete coverage, but only the more densely populated portions of Riverside and San Bernardino Counties are included on our maps. In order to preserve a sufficient scale to show detailed patterns across the entire map, we had to omit more distant, less populated areas. Thus, places farther north or east in the desert (e.g., Barstow, Banning, Hemet, Indio, and Palm Springs) are not shown. Maps also do not cover a narrow, sparsely populated zone along the western edge of Ventura County. However, when tables of population numbers and statistical results are reported for specific counties, we include the entire population of the counties.

No other counties in Southern California are covered. Although the San Diego and Santa Barbara areas are part of most people's conception of Southern California, those areas are too peripheral to be included. Moreover, San Diego—separated from Orange County by open hilly country and the Camp Pendleton Marine Base—is a very large and distinct metropolitan area in its own right.

Map preparation and design. Census 2000 data used in this book were downloaded from the Census Bureau's web site. Information needed for Southern California census tracts was extracted from the P.L. 94-171 Redistricting File and Summary File 1 for California. These data were joined to census tract boundary files in Environmental Systems Research Institute's (ESRI) ArcView 3.2 geographic information system (GIS) software. Resulting choropleth and dot maps were exported from Illustrator as *eps* files and then incorporated with the text in the Quark XPress 5.0 desktop publishing program.

The mapped data are shown by census tract, an areal unit of about 4000 persons created by the Census Bureau. Both choropleth and dot maps are used. Choropleth maps show by color the percentage that an ethnic group represents within each tract's total population. The tracts' percentage values are ranked from highest to lowest and that range is then divided into classes or categories that generally represent similar proportions. Depending on the nature of the percentage distributions, maps will have either five or six percentage categories.

We wished to highlight those tracts where the group was most strongly represented because in most cases these high-percentage tracts identify ethnic enclaves and institutional focuses for the group. For maps of Whites, Mexicans, Central Americans, percent owner-occupied housing, and diversity the highest category represents the top five percent of the tracts, the next category represents the next five percent, and the third category represents the next ten percent. For maps of Blacks, American Indians, Asians and Pacific Islanders, the five specific Asian groups, and persons of two or more races, the highest two categories represent the top five percent of the tracts. This is because the highest five percent of tracts covered such a large range of ethnic percentage values that the usual five-percent class was best split into two classes.

Because Census 2000 permitted respondents to mark more than one race, we made certain decisions regarding the treatment of mixed-race populations. Although proportionately small, the mixed-race numbers were apportioned fractionally into the component single-race groups for purposes of mapping. In the "New mixed-race data" section of chapter 2 we explain our straightforward but appropriate way to handle the dilemma posed by these data.

With respect to specific Asian groups, because the Chinese, Korean, Japanese, and Vietnamese are principally located in the more densely settled sections of Los Angeles and Orange Counties, their distributions are presented on quarter-page maps. In contrast, Filipinos are found in much greater numbers in Riverside, San Bernardino, and Ventura Counties, so that a full-page map is used for their distribution.

Dot maps are used to reveal increases or decreases in ethnic populations over the last decade. Tracts that realized a net gain were allocated a red dot for every 100 persons gained since 1990. Those that had a loss are shown by one blue dot for every 100 fewer persons in 2000. This method of mapping by red and blue dots clearly reveals where ethnic changes have occurred.

On the map of total population (Figure 3.1), we added shaded relief to indicate the major areas of hills and mountains. Knowing the locations of these less populated areas is important in understanding distributions. Shaded relief was not used on other maps because it would result in too many mixed and blurred colors.

That same map also uses three different dot values to better reveal the density of the underlying population since a single dot value typically results in either areas of solid, overlapping dots or large empty areas. Some experimentation led to our choice of break points of 10,000 and 25,000 persons per square mile between the different dot colors. This yielded a satisfactory dot pattern that also reveals where the population density is especially high.

Geographical terminology. In this book the Los Angeles metropolitan area always refers to the five-county region identified earlier in this chapter. Because some cities and counties have the same name, our references to county names always include the word "county". Thus, "Los Angeles, Riverside, and San Bernardino" refer to those cities. Like most local residents, we sometimes use "L.A." to refer to the city of Los Angeles.

The distinction between "older" as opposed to "newer" suburbs is useful in that it usually relates somewhat to differences in location, average housing cost, and ethnic composition. We consider suburbs that were built before about 1970 to be older ones. Use of 1970 as an approximate division between old and new makes sense because both economic restructuring and increased immigration began about that time.

Enclaves. The term "enclave" means a residential clustering or concentration of an ethnic population. We focus on enclaves because their relative strength is an important characteristic of both the ethnic group and the locality. In chapters 4, 5, and 6 we compare the percentage of each ethnic group that resided in enclaves in 1990 and 2000 as indicators of trends toward either increased spatial concentration or deconcentration for the group.

Residents of enclaves are not necessarily of lower economic status or less culturally assimilated than people living outside enclaves, although this has certainly been the typical situation in the United States, both for recent immigrants and for Blacks. Rather, some ethnic enclaves may be created voluntarily by the residents so as to promote the social, cultural, and economic benefits that come with larger group settlements.[13]

There is no consensus as to how such enclaves should be measured.[14] For smaller ethnic groups we defined enclaves as all census tracts in which the group is represented at three times or more its average percentage in the total five-county population. For the two largest groups—Latinos and Whites—we measured ethnic concentration by the percentages of the group residing in each of five categories of varying ethnic proportions within the total tract population.

Ethnic identity labels. In this book we generally use the federal government's categories and terminology for ethnic groups. The categories are socially meaningful today, and most ethnic category labels are easily understood. The widely used name "Latino" is now included by the government as a synonym for the term "Hispanic". Similarly, "African American" is now an official equivalent of "Black". For each of these groups the two terms are interchangeable, although we generally use "Latino" and "Black".

Most Whites do not identify themselves as such or with the older term "Caucasian". Rather, they say that they are simply Americans. Sometimes they identify with their religious heritage or with one or more national heritages, usually in Europe or the Middle East. However, because Whites are numerically large and have held most economic power, they are an especially important ethnic group and are treated as an ethnic group in this book. To keep other ethnic labels from becoming too cumbersome, we use "Pacific Islander" rather than the new federal government term, "Native Hawaiian and Other Pacific Islander".

The Census Bureau uses the term "ethnic" to refer particularly to groups included in the Hispanic or Latino tabulations and the term "race" to refer to the other categories we use in this book. However, we use the term "ethnic" to describe all the different populations in this book.

Because this book is oriented to ethnic identity rather than to immigration or country of birth, labels for groups include those born in the United States and others from another country. For example, "Mexican", "Black", and "Vietnamese" include both immigrants and members of the group born in the United States. When we need to distinguish immigrants from the American-born people in an ethnic group, the former are called "foreign-born" and latter, the "U.S.-born."

Acknowledgements

We appreciate the many individuals around Southern California who found *The Ethnic Quilt* useful and interesting and mentioned that they wished we could produce an update using the Census 2000 data. Their encouragement helped us carry out this new project. We hope that this book comes up to their expectations.

We asked experts on the various topics or ethnic groups covered in this book to read portions of our material and suggest improvements. Our thanks go to William A.V. Clark, Wei Li, Paul Robinson, Mary Pardo, Roberto Lovato, Joseph Holloway, and Karren Baird-Olson for giving us their insights in the form of this valuable feedback. Several excellent writers and editors in our CSUN Department of Geography helped us improve and correct earlier versions of the chapters. We appreciate very much the help that Bill Bowen, Darrick Danta, Robert Hoffpauir, Julie Laity, and Elliot McIntire provided in this regard. With respect to our concerns of Census 2000 data quality in neighborhoods, we were pleased to be able to work with Jeffrey Beckerman, demographer in the Los Angeles City Planning Department, and Javier Minjares of the Southern California Association of Governments (SCAG), and we thank them for assisting us.

Most photographs in our book were taken by Maria D. Ivey, who kindly used her expertise to provide us with photos of people in various places. David Deis of the Department of Geography Cartography Lab helped us with the shaded relief for the map of population distribution. Libby Roseman contributed the phrase "changing faces" for part of our book's title. A minigrant from the Research and Sponsored Projects Office of CSUN helped defray the cost of color printing of the maps. We continue to appreciate the support of the CSUN Center for Geographical Studies, our publisher. For the help generously provided by all of these, we are very grateful.

Lastly, we thank our loving wives, Nancy and Carol, for their continued support despite the long hours away from them that were required in order to research and produce this book.

Notes

1. The restructuring that Los Angeles and other metropolitan areas experienced from the late 1960s through the 1980s involved several components. The most important changes were the elimination of most high-paying manufacturing jobs that had been held by workers without advanced education and the creation of new jobs in services and in electronics and computer-related manufacturing. Service-sector employment became bifurcated into high-paying positions (in finance, law, insurance, health care, entertainment, real estate, etc.) for those with the required skills and low-paying jobs (in retail sales, lawn maintenance, office cleaning, dishwashing, and similar services) for those lacking sufficient education. These job shifts reflect technological improvements, the growing importance of well-educated workers, and an increasingly globalized economy. The first and perhaps still the best examination of urban economic restructuring in Los Angeles is Soja, Morales, and Wolff (1989).

2. Allen and Turner (1997). Another difference between the 1997 book and this one is the analyses of comparative ethnic socioeconomic status, or social class, in *The Ethnic Quilt*. No Census 2000 data on income, educational attainment, or occupation or other long-form census data were available to us in time for inclusion in this book. We indicate the 2000 geography of status or class only by a map of homeownership rates for of all households and a table of homeownership rates for the major ethnic groups. Because ethnic-class relationships and comparative positions usually do not change much during a decade, we refer interested readers to our analyses of 1990 census data in our earlier book.

3. In the last twenty years there has probably been more research and writing on Los Angeles than on any other metropolitan area in the country. A good introduction by a historian to much of the recent literature on Los Angeles is Engh (2000).

4. Kelley (1999).

5. This same five-county region is one of eighteen very large metropolitan areas in the United States that resulted from the coalescing of once separate metropolitan areas. Referring to it as the Los Angeles-Riverside-Orange County Consolidated Metropolitan Statistical Area (CMSA) distinguishes it from the Los Angeles–Long Beach Primary Metropolitan Statistical Area (PMSA), which includes only Los Angeles County. In federal data on primary metropolitan areas, Riverside and San Bernardino Counties are combined into a single PMSA, but Orange and Ventura Counties each constitute their own separate PMSAs.

6. To illustrate the comparative nature of much research on Los Angeles, employment decentralization in the Los Angeles CMSA was found to be quite typical of CMSAs (Gordon and Richardson 1996). Numerous articles in scholarly journals compare Los Angeles with other metropolitan areas. A recent detailed study of metropolitan Los Angeles shows how its spatial patterns illustrate much wider urban processes (Soja 2000). Similarly, a book edited by Waldinger (2001) contains chapters that compare Los Angeles with other large metropolitan areas with regard to the situation and progress of immigrants.

7. Garreau (1991), 3.

8. Gordon and Richardson (1998), 104.

9. Gordon and Richardson (1998), 105.

10. Clark (2000); Gottdiener and Kephart (1991); Gordon et al. (1986).

11. Garreau (1991), 430-431; Giuliano and Small (1991).

12. The traditional spatial assimilation model was most thoroughly explained by Massey (1985) and is widely used in urban ethnic research, especially in sociology. We tested the traditional model in Southern California as of 1990 and suggested modifications based on that test (Allen and Turner 1996b).

13. Our perspective that enclaves may be either advantageous and positive or disadvantageous and negative is consistent with Marcuse (1997), Kempen and Ozuekren (1998), and Logan, Alba, and Zhang (2002). In contrast, social scientists have traditionally viewed enclaves as necessarily bad: enclaves reflect poverty, low levels of education, constraints on housing mobility, and sometimes White discrimination against minorities. Also, the concept of "enclave" as used here does not imply any necessary ethnic business activities in the area, as it does in certain sociology contexts.

14. Our methods of measuring enclaves are similar to those developed by Poulsen, Forrest, and Johnston (2002).

2. Census 2000 Data

The information that is mapped in this book was collected by the U.S. Census Bureau in March and April, 2000. It is the latest in the series of censuses required every ten years by the federal constitution. Although it is not perfect, it is the most detailed and generally best data available on the American people. With advances in technology, these and a vast array of other data can be viewed or downloaded conveniently from the U.S. Census Bureau's web site, http://www.census.gov. Because all the 2000 data in this book is 100-percent-count data, taken from the short-form of the census, our maps and tables do not have any sampling error.

Race and Hispanic data. In recent censuses respondents have indicated their ethnic identity on two separate questions—one with listed "race" categories and the other for Hispanic or Latino identity. Racial and Hispanic identities and populations are thus separated by the Census Bureau. Latinos and other people of Hispanic heritage can be of any race. However, we use cross tabulations of these data in order to distinguish the socially more important identities and, in some cases, to avoid double counting of persons.

We include as Whites only those who were not Latino or Hispanic. This is the group sometimes called "Anglos". Our use of this "non-Hispanic White" group follows general practice among social scientists. Similarly, for Blacks we use data only for non-Hispanic Blacks. This is because, in our judgment, most people who are both Black and Hispanic have stronger identities as Hispanic.[1] This procedure enabled all White Hispanics and Black Hispanics to be counted fully as part of the Hispanic or Latino population while avoiding double counting of individuals. On the other hand, for American Indians and Asian and Pacific Islanders who had some Hispanic heritage, we consider the Hispanic identity to be secondary. Thus, we avoid double counting by including Hispanic American Indians and Hispanic Asians and Pacific Islanders in their race group totals but subtracting them from the Hispanic totals.

Changes in Census Procedures

In this book we frequently compare 1990 and 2000 numbers to show change in different ethnic populations. For this reason, changes in Census Bureau procedures from one census to the next can affect apparent trends.

Hispanic or Latino nationalities. The total number of Hispanics or Latinos counted in Census 2000 appears to have been excellent and perhaps even a bit more complete than in the 1990 census. However, the 2000 counts of specific Latino groups were much lower than expected, prompting widespread discussion and concern.[2] The discrepancy may well have resulted from changes in census questionnaire wording, the most important of which was the omission in Census 2000 of specific Hispanic nationality examples such as "Argentinean, Salvadoran" below the line on which respondents were asked to write in their specific identity.[3] An analysis by the Census Bureau has shown that these changes were significant in some of the Hispanic nationality counts.[4] Another possible factor behind the reduced counts could be a greater acceptance of a Hispanic or Latino identity, such that specific Hispanic nationality identities weakened during the 1990s. In California, where the word "Latino" is widely accepted, the fact that the word "Latino" was included with "Spanish" and "Hispanic" on the basic Hispanic question in Census 2000 may have increased acceptance of this broader identity.[5] Whatever the cause, measuring trends for specific nationality groups by comparing 1990 and 2000 census figures is problematic.

Because the Census 2000 counts of specific Hispanic nationalities seem so low, the Pew Hispanic Center developed a methodology to produce estimates of Hispanic nationalities that we believe are superior to the Census counts.[6] Accordingly, in Table 5.1 we supplement Census 2000 figures with those estimates. However, the Pew Center's methodology was not intended to generate estimates for small areas like tracts.

The weakness of the 2000 tract data on Latino nationalities meant that maps of change for Mexicans and Central Americans would be less reliable. However, the map of Hispanic change 1990-2000 (Figure 5.1) is based on the total Hispanic count, which is widely accepted. Maps of percent Mexican and percent Central American (Figures 5.2 and 5.3) use the Census 2000 data because the relative patterns are well portrayed although percentage values are presumably too low.

New mixed-race data. For the first time in the history of the U.S. census, questionnaires permitted people to check more than one of the identities listed in the question concerning race. This is an appropriate change in that it recognizes the many Americans of mixed racial heritage and the rapidly increasing number of biracial children from racially mixed marriages. Nevertheless, only 4.7 percent of Californians marked more than one race.[7]

The new data pose difficulties in analysis. Measuring ethnic population change since 1990 is problematic because it is not clear whether each group should include only those who reported that identity alone or should also include those who reported both that identity and another. Also, some groups are much more multiracial. Nationwide about 40 percent of American Indians and over 50 percent of Pacific Islanders marked two or more races. Thus, the American Indian and Alaska Native population could be said to have grown by either 26 percent or 110 percent during the 1990s depending on whether people reporting some other race as well as American Indian are included for 2000.

Many researchers face this problem of how best to "bridge" or make comparable the 1990 and 2000 race data sets. The federal government's Office of Management and Budget has investigated carefully the options and presents these on its web site.[8]

We believe the best practical solution for bridging and mapping purposes is a fractional assignment or apportionment of the mixed-race populations into the appropriate single-race groups. Assigning mixed-race people in equal fractions to each of the race groups they marked is reasonable, and we do this with the mixed-American Indian populations. However, our research suggests an improvement is possible in some cases. For example, we determined that in California 67.1 percent of the mixed Black-White population identified their race as Black in 1990.[9] Similarly, 32.8 percent of California's mixed Asian-White population in 1990 identified their race as Asian. In this book we use those same percentages to apportion the mixed White-Black and White-Asian numbers in each tract to each of those race groups. This method for fractionally assigning the larger mixed-race populations ensures that our maps and tables of 1990-2000 change will minimize any possible bias due to the new mixed-race data in Census 2000. The effect of this fractional assignment is very small, but this procedure ensures that people of multiracial identity will not be forgotten or wrongly assigned to only one of their identities.

The method of fractional assignment could not be used to apportion mixed-race people in specific Asian groups, such as Chinese or Japanese, because census tabulations did not specify the other race of those individuals. Thus, maps of Asian groups represent a small degree of undercount because they are based on only those individuals who checked a single race.

Changes in census tract boundaries.

For over half a century the Census Bureau has used the census tract as the areal unit designed to represent the neighborhood. Difficulties occur, however, in mapping change over time because some tract boundaries are shifted between censuses.

Inconsistencies in tract boundaries must be dealt with one at a time. We resolved these matters by aggregating 1990 blocks into 2000 tracts so that 1990 populations could be calculated for the more numerous 2000 tracts. Where 2000 tracts split 1990 blocks, the boundaries were examined in detail to determine which tract should receive the block population.

Census Undercounting and Errors

The undercount and map patterns.

Although the Census Bureau attempted to count all residents of the United States, some people are always missed. It is clear that minorities are more likely than Whites to be missed. The ethnic differential in rates of census coverage has been very disturbing to the Bureau and to many Americans.

It appears that the net undercount in 2000 was much less than in 1990, both for Blacks and for non-Blacks.[10] Rates of net undercount estimated by the Census Bureau for the five counties of the Los Angeles CMSA ranged from a low of 1.07 percent in Ventura County to a high of 1.81 percent in Los Angeles County.[11] However, the methods of estimating undercount are fraught with assumptions and data quality problems so that net undercount estimates can be only approximations.

The total population of various counties and cities is affected by any undercount, but in small areas like census tracts the problem becomes much less significant. The people who were omitted in the census were presumably widely distributed across many neighborhoods.

Census errors in specific tracts.

What can be significant, however, are any census errors that affect some neighborhoods or tracts much more than others. Such errors can be particularly noticeable when total population change between 1990 and 2000 is mapped.

The most egregious Census Bureau errors involved the misplacement of certain group-quarters populations in tracts adjacent to their correct location. Group-quarters populations are people who live, not in households, but rather in prisons, college dorms, mental hospitals, or similar group settings.

After investigation to determine which group-quarters losses were real and which resulted from misplacement, we corrected the erroneous group-quarter locations in our digital files. These involved 7,113 prisoners in the Peter Pitchess Detention Center in Castaic (tract 9202); 918 patients at the Metropolitan State Hospital in Norwalk (tract 5500); 2,500 college students in dorms at the University of Southern California (tract 2227); 1,200 students at California State Polytechnic University, Pomona (tract 4024.04); and the 1990 misplacement of 1,400 students at California State University, Northridge (tract 1152.02). Such errors were widespread nationally.[12]

There may have been other tract-level errors. After investigation we found one tract with such a serious error that it deserves mention here. Tract 2742, the upper-income Venice Beach peninsula in Los Angeles City (adjacent to Marina del Rey), did not, in fact, lose population during the 1990s despite the fact that the count from Census 2000 was lower by about 1,600 housing units and 2,500 persons. Because we did not have the information to correct this error completely, it appears on the map of White population change as wrongly indicating a large White population decrease.

Notes

1. This is the view expressed by Nancy Foner, Professor of Anthropology at the State University of New York at Purchase, in personal conversation. Foner is an expert on West Indian migrations to New York City. Although we recognize that most Americans view Black Hispanics as essentially Black rather than Hispanic, self-identification as Hispanic seems more important in this case.

2. Fields (2001).

3. The 1990 census questionnaire asked Hispanic-origin people for their specific national origin group. Mexican, Cuban, and Puerto Rican identities were specifically listed so that people with any of those identities could check the appropriate circle. For other national identities, the questionnaire asked people to write this under the category "other Spanish/Hispanic", and the names of six groups were given to encourage respondents to fill in that space with their nationality if appropriate.

On the Census 2000 questionnaire, the word "Latino" was added as an equivalent to "Spanish/Hispanic" and the word "origin" was omitted. Thus, in 2000 respondents were asked "Is Person 1 Spanish/Hispanic/Latino?" instead of the 1990 version, "Is this person of Spanish/Hispanic origin?" In addition, in Census 2000 no examples of other Hispanic nationalities were provided as prompts to encourage nationality write-ins. Where the directions said to "Print group", some people might not have realized that the Census Bureau wanted specific nationality groups.

4. Martin (2002).

5. In Los Angeles the adoption of a Latino identity on the part of many children of Salvadoran and Guatemalan immigrants is explained in Hamilton and Chinchilla (2001), 56.

6. Suro (2002). The report estimated specific Hispanic nationality totals for 2000, using data from the Census 2000 Supplementary Survey (C2SS) that was based on a national sample of 700,000 households. Earlier, sociologist John Logan derived another set of estimates from Current Population Survey data from the Census Bureau (Logan 2001b).

7. U.S. Census Bureau (2001f).

8. U.S. Office of Management and Budget (2000).

9. Allen and Turner (2001), Table 9. Our research was based on separate nationwide and California analyses of race and ancestry identities of individuals using the Public Use Microdata Sample File of the 1990 census. Individuals whose race and write-in ancestry identities represented different races were considered biracial. The identity chosen for the race question was considered the primary identity of mixed-race people. We calculated the percentage of each mixed-race group that chose one, as opposed to the other, as their primary identity. We then applied these percentages to the 2000 mixed-race populations in Southern California.

10. U.S. Census Bureau (2001e).

11. U.S. Census Bureau (2001g).

12. Scott (2001).

3. Getting Oriented

Understanding map patterns requires that the reader be oriented to the area covered. This is the purpose of the map of total population, on which the more rugged hills and mountains are shown in shading (Figure 3.1). Next, a map and table showing the varying percentages of homeownership in the region make use of the only socioeconomic data from Census 2000 that are available in time for this publication (Figure 3.2; Table 3.1). Lastly, we provide a brief historical orientation to the changes in ethnic composition experienced over the last forty years (Figure 3.3; Table 3.2).

Population Distribution and Terrain

Variations in population density are shown by both different colors of dots and the relative clustering or dispersion of the dots (Figure 3.1), as explained in chapter 1 under "Map preparation and design". The highest density neighborhoods shown in red contain multi-unit residential structures—apartments or condominiums. Most but not all of the areas represented are in poor areas, and some tracts in the most densely settled area west of Downtown Los Angeles have over 60,000 residents per square mile.

Less dense areas, indicated by the orange-yellow dots, may be older suburbs where single-family houses are small and close together. This is particularly evident in the large area south of Downtown. The same color may also represent more affluent neighborhoods if they contain many apartment buildings, as along the coast at Santa Monica and Long Beach. The pale-yellow dots indicate less densely settled areas, usually newer suburbs with few large apartment buildings or condo complexes.

Noticeable areas of gaps between the dots indicate non-residential areas. Some of these are highly urban, such as Los Angeles International Airport (LAX), industrial areas southeast of Downtown L.A. (e.g., the city of Vernon) and northwest of Long Beach, large parks like Griffith Park north of Downtown L.A., and river flood control basins in the San Fernando and San Gabriel Valleys. A few large areas represent undeveloped country surrounded by already developed suburbs: the Ahmanson Ranch land in Ventura County just west of the San Fernando Valley and a large remnant of the former Irvine Ranch property in Orange County.

Areas of widely scattered dots indicate a rural population or new suburban developments adjacent to farmland, desert, or otherwise undeveloped country. The largest remaining farm areas are in two locations. One is the section of Riverside and San Bernardino Counties that is west of Interstate 15 and south of Route 60; the other is in Ventura County east of Oxnard. To the north of the San Gabriel Mountains is the Mojave Desert, which includes the Antelope Valley west and east of the cities of Lancaster and Palmdale and the Victor Valley around Victorville. The same low-density situation occurs in the semi-desert of Riverside County south of Corona and Perris, where new suburbs are sometimes close to farmland.

The largest non-residential areas on the map represent mountainous country. Most of this is in the Los Padres and Angeles National Forests that are controlled by the federal government. We have added shaded relief to help make clear the areas of steep-sloped terrain. By far the largest area is the San Gabriel Mountains, which separate the Los Angeles Basin and San Gabriel and San Bernardino Valleys from the desert to the north. Cajon Pass, at the eastern end of the San Gabriel Mountains, provides an important highway and railroad route between Southern California and points east. West of the San Gabriel Mountains is the rugged but lower-elevation Sierra Pelona and the even more wild Sespe country of northern Ventura County west of Interstate 5. The boundary between Orange and Riverside Counties lies in the rugged Santa Ana Mountains within Cleveland National Forest.

Smaller areas of hills and mountains closer to urban areas are often more significant to local residents. For example, the Verdugo Mountains separate the San Fernando Valley from a narrow valley to the east. Privately owned land in the more centrally located hills has often been built up with expensive homes. This has occurred in the Santa Monica Mountains, which trend east-west behind the Malibu coast and separate the San Fernando Valley from the Los Angeles Basin.

These terrain features have strongly influenced settlement in Southern California and should be taken into account when interpreting the maps in this book.

Patterns of Homeownership

While most Americans and immigrants seek to own their own home, many must rent because they do not have the money or credit to buy. Rates of homeownership in the four counties surrounding Los Angeles County range from 61 percent in Orange County to 69 percent in Riverside County.[1] Due to higher-priced housing and a lower proportion of households with higher incomes, the homeownership rate in Los Angeles County is only 46 percent.

The older, more central areas of cities have generally lower rates of homeownership because the lower rents for both apartments and single-family houses in such areas attract poorer people (Figure 3.2). The largest such area is in and near Downtown Los Angeles, but even much smaller cities show the predominance of renters in their central sections.

Homeownership is most common in areas of affluence, such as most of the Santa Monica Mountains, Redlands, San Marino, Mission Viejo, and La Habra Heights. Many developments in outlying suburbs also have high rates of homeownership, as in the new sections of Santa Clarita, Thousand Oaks, Fontana, Corona, and the Orange County settlements between routes 55 and 241.

Rates of homeownership are usually very low in tracts that are dominated by industry and office buildings, some of which are sufficiently large to be easily seen on the map. This characterizes several tracts southeast of Downtown L.A. and others in El Segundo, Wilmington, and Long Beach. A large tract in

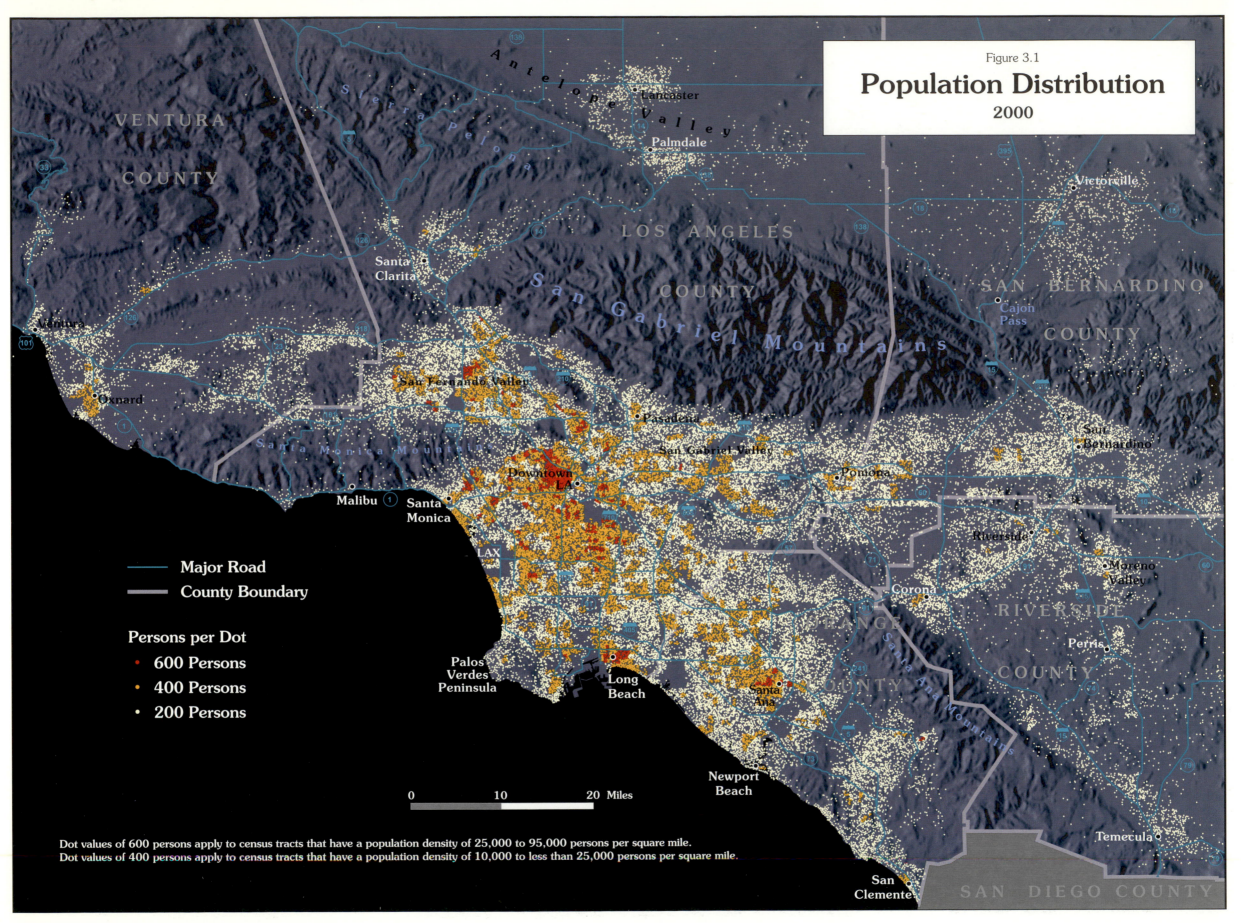

Figure 3.1
Population Distribution
2000

Major Road

County Boundary

Persons per Dot

- 600 Persons
- 400 Persons
- 200 Persons

Dot values of 600 persons apply to census tracts that have a population density of 25,000 to 95,000 persons per square mile.
Dot values of 400 persons apply to census tracts that have a population density of 10,000 to less than 25,000 persons per square mile.

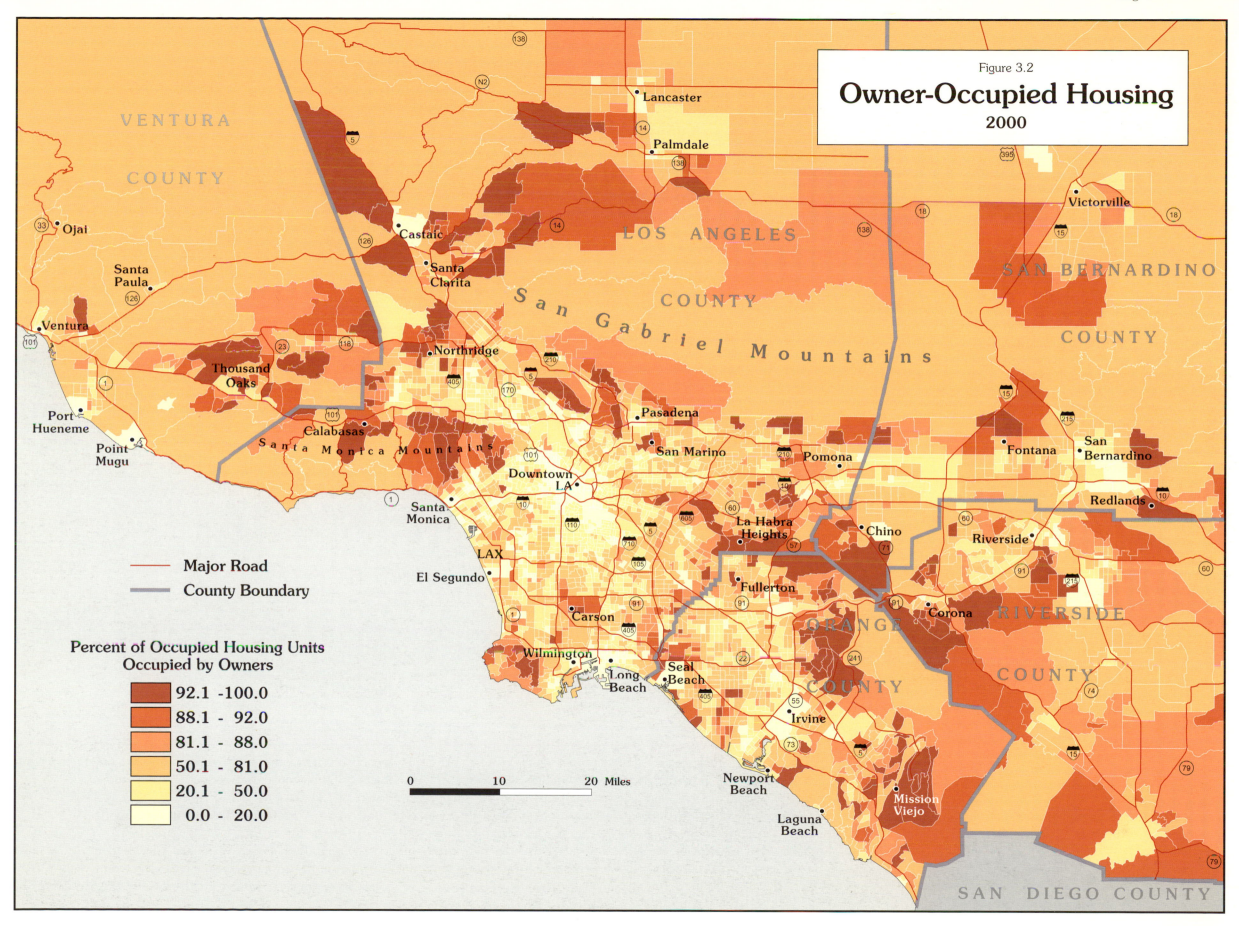

Figure 3.2
Owner-Occupied Housing
2000

Major Road
County Boundary

Percent of Occupied Housing Units
Occupied by Owners

92.1 - 100.0
88.1 - 92.0
81.1 - 88.0
50.1 - 81.0
20.1 - 50.0
0.0 - 20.0

0   10   20 Miles

Irvine and Tustin that is almost completely occupied by office complexes, high-tech manufacturing plants, and a former U.S. Marine Corps helicopter station similarly appears as having very low homeownership.

In addition, military facilities have very low rates of homeownership. Evident on the map because of their size are former military installations—George Air Force Base northwest of Victorville and March Air Force Base southeast of Riverside—as well as active U.S. Navy stations at Seal Beach, Port Hueneme, and Point Mugu. Large tracts in which most residents live in group quarters rather than in individual housing units are also shown in the lowest homeownership category. On the map the most visible tracts contain large prisons—Los Angeles County's Peter Pitchess Detention Center in Castaic and the California state prisons in Chino and west of Lancaster.

Ethnic homeownership rates and change. Because homeownership is an important social and economic indicator of successful economic adaptation, rates and trends can be illuminating as to the status of groups. (Table 3.1).

The fact that White and Asian households are most likely to be homeowners is of no surprise, considering their much higher average incomes (Table 7.3). In addition, White homeownership is particularly high because many older Whites bought their first home decades ago, at a time when housing prices were much lower than now.

Table 3.1. Percent Homeowners, 1990 and 2000: Los Angeles CMSA

Ethnic Group	1990	2000
White	61.8	64.8
Latino	38.9	42.7
Black	37.5	39.0
Asian and Pacific Islander	54.2	53.7
American Indian	44.7	44.9

Sources: U.S. Census Bureau 1992, 2002a.

Notes: Percentages are calculated from all occupied housing units; all of these not occupied by the owner are considered rentals. Figures for 2000 for race groups include only households where the householder reported a single race.

Most ethnic groups increased their rates of homeownership during the 1990s. Homeownership increased most among Latinos, suggesting significant progress economically. Interpretation of trends is difficult, however, because ethnic groups may have differed in the proportions of new immigrants and lower-income households migrating into or out of the region during the 1990s. Some such differential migration, perhaps related to the 45-percent growth in numbers of foreign-born from Asia in 2000 compared to 1990, may explain the small decline in Asian and Pacific Islander homeownership.[2]

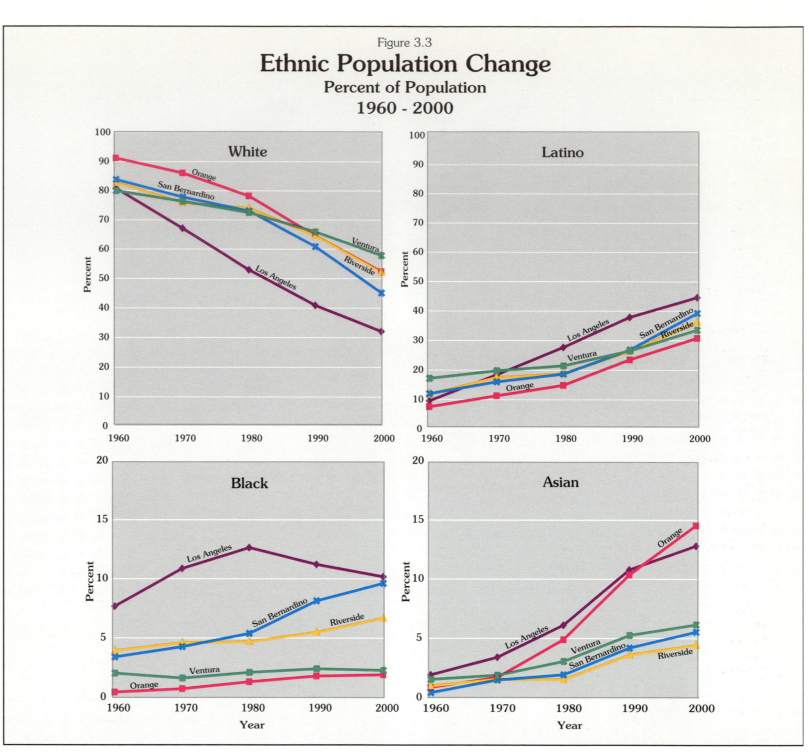

Figure 3.3
Ethnic Population Change
Percent of Population
1960 - 2000

Separate analyses for each county as of 2000 (not shown here) indicate that the highest rate of homeownership for all groups except Asians and Pacific Islanders is in Riverside County, where recently built homes have sold at relatively low prices. Among Latinos, homeownership is widespread in both Riverside County (58.8 percent) and San Bernardino County (59.8 percent). On the other hand, Ventura County has a higher Asian and Pacific Islander homeownership rate (70.0 percent) than any other county, and Ventura County is second highest in homeownership for both Whites and Blacks.

Ethnic Transformation

During the last forty years Los Angeles County, the most populous in the United States, increased by more than 50 percent. More dramatic, however, has been the growth of the four

Table 3.2. Ethnic Populations, 1960-2000: Counties in Los Angeles CMSA

	(Numbers in 000's)					Percent Change			
Los Angeles County									
	1960	1970	1980	1990	2000	1960-70	1970-80	1980-90	1990-00
Whites	4,877	4,717	3,954	3,619	3,049	-3	-16	-9	-16
Blacks	462	763	944	993	967	65	24	5	-3
Latinos	577	1,289	2,066	3,351	4,242	123	60	62	27
Asians	115	238	455	954	1,217	107	91	110	28
American Indians	8	25	48	46	106	213	92	-4	130
Total	6,039	7,032	7,478	8,863	9,519	16	6	19	7
Orange County									
	1960	1970	1980	1990	2000	1960-70	1970-80	1980-90	1990-00
Whites	642	1,222	1,511	1,555	1,488	90	24	3	-4
Blacks	3	10	25	43	54	233	150	72	26
Latinos	53	160	286	565	876	202	79	98	55
Asians	6	24	94	249	413	300	292	165	66
American Indians	1	4	13	12	28	300	225	-8	133
Total	704	1,420	1,933	2,411	2,846	102	36	25	18
Riverside County									
	1960	1970	1980	1990	2000	1960-70	1970-80	1980-90	1990-00
Whites	253	348	490	754	803	38	41	54	7
Blacks	12	21	31	64	103	75	48	107	61
Latinos	36	80	124	308	560	122	55	148	82
Asians	3	7	10	42	68	133	43	320	62
American Indians	2	3	8	12	25	50	167	50	108
Total	306	459	663	1,170	1,545	50	44	77	32
San Bernardino County									
	1960	1970	1980	1990	2000	1960-70	1970-80	1980-90	1990-00
Whites	422	532	653	862	769	26	23	32	-11
Blacks	17	29	48	115	164	71	66	140	43
Latinos	60	109	166	379	669	82	52	128	77
Asians	2	10	17	59	94	400	70	247	59
American Indians	2	3	12	13	28	50	300	8	115
Total	504	684	895	1,418	1,709	36	31	58	21
Ventura County									
	1960	1970	1980	1990	2000	1960-70	1970-80	1980-90	1990-00
Whites	159	287	383	441	435	81	33	15	-1
Blacks	4	6	11	16	17	50	83	46	6
Latinos	34	74	113	177	252	118	53	57	42
Asians	3	7	16	35	46	133	129	119	31
American Indians	0.2	1	6	5	10	400	500	-17	100
Total	199	376	529	670	753	89	41	27	12
Total in Los Angeles CMSA									
	1960	1970	1980	1990	2000	1960-70	1970-80	1980-90	1990-00
Whites	6,353	7,106	6,991	7,231	6,544	12	-2	3	-10
Blacks	498	829	1,059	1,231	1,305	67	28	16	6
Latinos	760	1,712	2,755	4,780	6,599	125	61	74	38
Asians	129	286	592	1,339	1,838	122	107	126	37
American Indians	13	36	87	88	197	177	142	1	124
Total	7,753	9,969	11,484	14,669	16,483	29	15	28	12

Sources: Selected U.S. Census publications and digital files.

Notes: Asians includes Pacific Islanders. American Indians includes Alaska Natives. Numbers are rounded to the nearest thousand.
Totals for 2000 include fractionally assigned mixed-race populations (chap. 2). Whites are only non-Hispanic Whites, but American Indians, Blacks, and Asians who identified also as Hispanic are counted fully in both the Hispanic (Latino) group and their race group. Because of this and other problems of ethnic categorization in various censuses, the ethnic numbers in this table do not sum exactly to the total official population counts from the U.S. censuses.

outlying or suburban counties. Each of those tripled in population since 1960.

As part of these growth patterns, the change in ethnic composition of Southern California has been dramatic (Figure 3.3). In all counties White proportions have declined substantially and Latino proportions increased. In all the counties, Blacks and Asians are far outnumbered by Latinos.

The higher Asian percentages in Los Angeles and Orange Counties and lower Black percentages in Orange and Ventura Counties are real differences. They reflect significant ethnic differences in preferred destinations.

A table of absolute numbers in each group—as opposed to percentages—in the five counties can also illuminate patterns and trends (Table 3.2). For example, Whites in Los Angeles County have been declining in numbers each decade since 1960, when many began to move to Orange County and other outlying areas. In the 1990s Whites decreased in numbers for the first time in Orange, San Bernardino, and Ventura Counties (Figure 3.4). If that trend and the rapid growth of Latino populations continue, Latinos will soon outnumber Whites in the outlying counties as they now do in Los Angeles County.

Los Angeles County has long been the center of the Black community in Southern California, but many Blacks have been moving to newer suburbs in Riverside and San Bernardino Counties.

Immigration from Asian and Pacific Island countries has resulted in a rapid growth of Asian numbers in Southern California, particularly in Los Angeles and Orange Counties.

Clearly the ethnic mix of people in Southern California has changed dramatically. In the 1960s most residents were recognizably White, with Blacks and Latinos much less common and living usually in certain neighborhoods. By 2002 the people of Southern California—whether on the streets, in shopping centers, at schools, or in religious congregations—were much less likely to be White.

The long-term meaning of this transformation of ethnic composition and physical appearance is not known but the subject of much discussion. Estimating the significance of the ethnic change is difficult because shifts of ethnic proportions are only one component of change in the region; and various cultural, economic, and political processes are interrelated with ethnic change in complex ways.

Notes

1. These Census 2000 figures and others in this book not referenced are from the American Factfinder section of the Census Bureau's website. http://factfinder.census.gov

2. U.S. Census Bureau (1993d, Table 28); U.S. Census Bureau (2002c, Table DP-2).

4. Whites and Blacks

This chapter builds on the data and generalizations about White and Black change that were introduced near the end of chapter 3. Table 3.2 reports ethnic population totals and rates of change for counties and the five-county region. This chapter, in contrast, explores both distributions and ethnic change at a much more geographically detailed scale—in neighborhoods and larger localities.

Because this book focuses on contemporary distributions of groups and changes that occurred during the 1990s, we do not attempt here to explain the historical geography of White and Black settlement in Los Angeles. That was covered in *The Ethnic Quilt*. We do, however, include key aspects of the history where these help explain patterns.

This chapter does not cover the heritage of White racism toward Blacks, once so blatant in Southern California and in other parts of the United States. Such attitudes have by no means disappeared, although they have weakened substantially. We do, however, discuss here and in chapter 7 the continued significance of attitudes toward other groups, racial discrimination in the housing market, and ethnic differences in economic resources because these factors do affect the changing distributions of groups.

White Population Change

Net White decline in Southern California. During the 1990s the number of Whites in the five-county region declined by over 690,000. Each of the counties except Riverside lost Whites. The greatest decline by far was in Los Angeles County, where 570,000 fewer Whites were counted in 2000 than in 1990.

Whites have been leaving the older and more central parts of Los Angeles County for several decades. L.A. County's White population dropped by a quarter between 1960 and 1990, but during the 1990s this net White loss became more widespread (Figure 4.1). Whites continued to move to suburbs,

especially to recently developed tracts closer to the fringe of the metropolitan area.

Orange County illustrates the trend. Whereas Whites increased by 13 percent during the 1970s, their growth was much less in the 1980s—2.5 percent. This was because the larger White numbers leaving the county came closer to balancing those moving in. Then, during the 1990s the net flow was reversed as the number of Whites in Orange County declined by 3 percent.

Most of this White decline in all counties except Riverside resulted from net out-migration. Some Whites moved to other parts of California, but more migrated to states in the Western United States such as Arizona, Nevada, and Oregon or to states in the East and South.

People probably left Southern California for the same reasons as in earlier decades—increased congestion, high home prices, fear of crime, and discomfort with growing ethnic minority populations. In addition, during the first half of the 1990s many people lost their jobs in the severe recession set off by the downturn in defense spending, which hit Southern California's aerospace industry particularly hard.

White decreases in older neighborhoods. The location of clusters of blue dots makes it clear that Whites were especially moving out of older neighborhoods, often where housing was modest and less expensive than in newer developments. This can be seen in the Oxnard and Simi Valley areas of Ventura County and in the older parts of Ontario, Rialto, San Bernardino, Corona, and Riverside. Similarly, in the San Fernando Valley, White decline was much less in the more affluent Santa Monica Mountain neighborhoods south of the 101 Freeway than elsewhere.

Perhaps the clearest example of this pattern is in Orange County. The northern half of the county was developed mostly in the 1950s and 1960s as new suburbs primarily for Whites, but by the 1980s and 1990s many Whites were forsaking these older

neighborhoods for newer homes in Orange or Riverside County or elsewhere.

Many observers have wondered to what extent such White departures have been motivated by the economics of investing in newer housing, by such factors as the reputation of local schools and school districts, or by discomfort with growing minority populations. Because most people consider both economic and social reasons when they make decisions on where to live, this question can probably never be answered.

White increases in the suburbs. White population growth has tended to be in outlying areas where most newer housing developments have been located. Frequently these new developments have scenic mountain or canyon views, or they are on gentle slopes above older homes and towns on flatter land below.

For example, many Whites who left northern Orange County moved to newer cities like Laguna Hills or Mission Viejo. Others settled closer to the Santa Ana Mountains, in wild mountain country of Cleveland National Forest, sometimes on unincorporated county territory in places like Portola Hills or Trabuco Canyon. Some people found lower home prices by going over the mountains to Riverside County, where several new tracts west of Interstate 15 offer dramatic views of the adjacent rugged Santa Ana Range. Even closer to nature is rapidly growing Crestline—a town nestled within the San Bernardino Mountains.

The shortage of land for building new homes in Los Angeles County and northern Orange County and the lower price of land in more distant places mean that new, less expensive homes are usually built near the periphery of the metropolitan area. Such places include new developments west of Palmdale in northern Los Angeles County; newer sections of Fontana, Rancho Cucamonga, Chino Hills, Victorville, and Hesperia in San Bernardino County; and Murrieta, Temecula, and Corona in Riverside County.

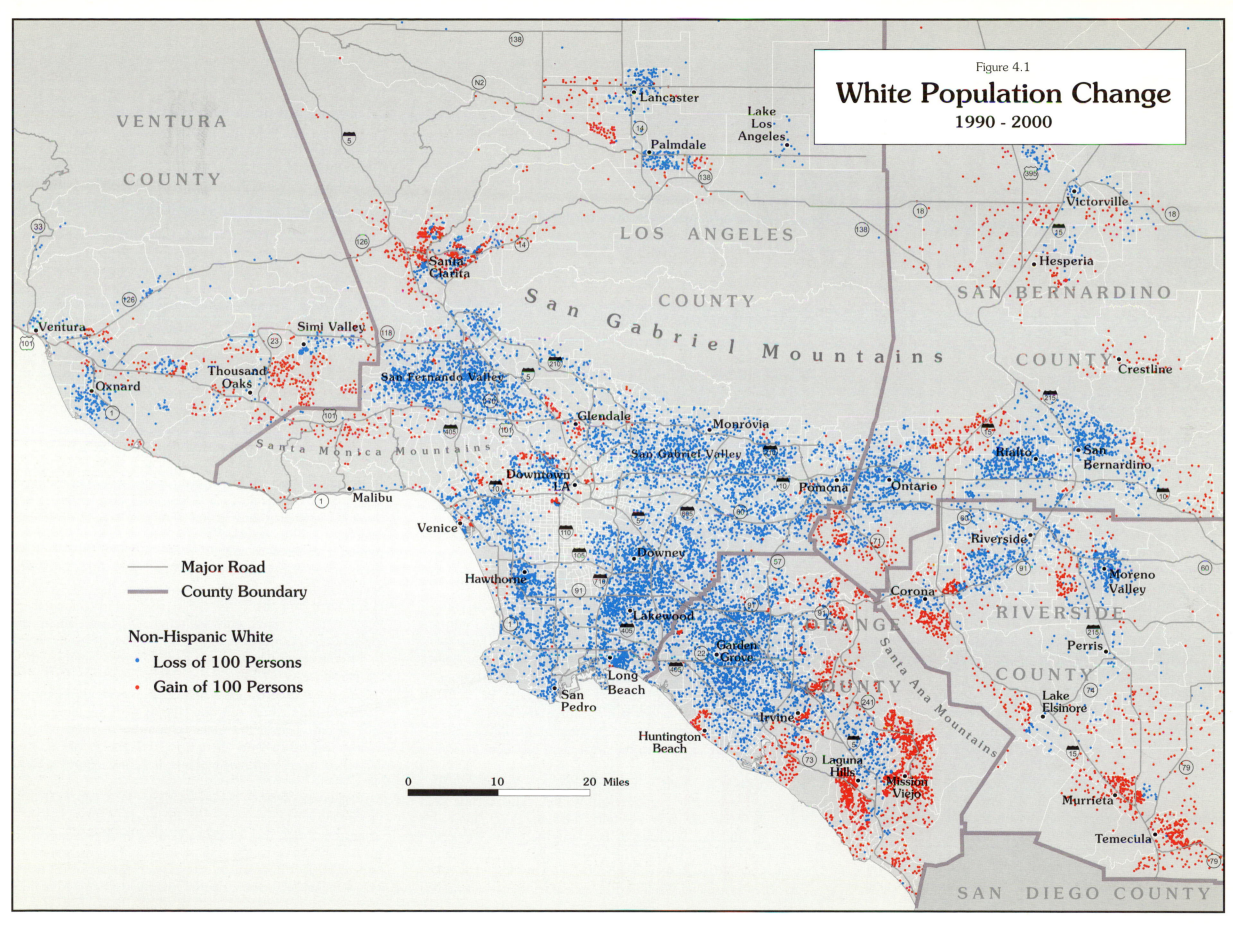

Figure 4.1
White Population Change
1990 - 2000

Major Road

County Boundary

Non-Hispanic White
• Loss of 100 Persons
• Gain of 100 Persons

0   10   20 Miles

Hancock Park, Westside Los Angeles

On the average, new housing that is closer to the larger Los Angeles area employment centers has been more expensive. Thus, White population increases in Santa Clarita, Calabasas, Malibu, Thousand Oaks, Camarillo, Irvine, Huntington Beach, Newport Beach, and Southern Orange County in general represent the more affluent Whites.

A few areas of affluent Malibu experienced the opposite of the usual pattern of White gain. The decrease of Whites during the 1990s in certain parts of that city resulted from the loss of hundreds of homes in the devastating fire of November, 1993.

Pockets of White increases in older areas. In some older neighborhoods special attractions led to growth in numbers of Whites. This is contrary to the general White population losses expected from older residential areas. Any of three factors could have been involved, but the particular factors involved with any such change can only be known by investigation into the specific neighborhoods.

One reason for White increases in older areas has been residential in-filling. This is where new apartments or single-family houses are built on land previously vacant or used for purposes other than housing. In some neighborhoods older houses or apartments have been demolished to make way for the new housing. Most of the small pockets of White increase in older settled areas of Los Angeles and Orange County probably result from such new construction.

Closely related to in-filling is gentrification, which can also bring White growth in older neighborhoods. Gentrification occurs when affluent people (usually Whites) buy old, architecturally interesting but often deteriorating houses in older, lower-priced, more central neighborhoods—the neighborhoods that most Whites abandoned to Blacks or others decades earlier.

These newcomers then renovate their houses. If these changes occur with many houses, an upgrading of the neighborhood can occur. Previous renters in the area may be forced out by the increase in housing prices. Such gentrified neighborhoods are usually not far from centers of employment and entertainment, such as Downtown Los Angeles.

Gentrification may explain some White increases in more central neighborhoods, but the number of people involved is small. Although gentrification has been occurring in Angelino Heights (north of Downtown) and the West Adams area (west of Downtown), the trend is barely evident on the map (Figure 4.1).

Immigration and ethnic resettlement are the likely factors behind White growth in those localities where White ethnic enclaves are located.[1] Iranians (Persians) have a business center in the Westwood area of Los Angeles, Russian immigrants congregate in part of West Hollywood, and Armenians have found Glendale particularly attractive.

In the western and southern portions of Glendale, the clusters of White population growth can probably best be explained by an influx of Armenians. The Glendale Armenian enclave is well known, and it attracts Armenians from many countries, such as Iran, Lebanon, Armenia, and Russia. Some Armenians have moved to Glendale from East Hollywood, a much poorer area where many settled when they first arrived as refugees or immigrants.

Varying White Proportions

Although a half century ago Whites were the leading ethnic group in the more central areas of many large cities, White departure for the suburbs has meant that these places have few Whites today (Figure 4.2). Relatively low White percentages cover a very large area in the city of Los Angeles, but the same situation is found in the more central parts of Long Beach and Santa Ana. During decades when racial tensions were particularly high, White flight from Blacks was an important motivation to leave, in addition to the usual more economic reasons prompting suburbanization.

On the other hand, some urban areas are heavily White because they remain attractive to Whites. This is true of Redlands in San Bernardino County, east Long Beach, most of Pasadena, and the Westside of Los Angeles. (The Westside includes the cities of Beverly Hills, West Hollywood, and Santa Monica, as well as sections of Los Angeles City like Hancock Park, Brentwood, and Westwood.) Demand for these residential

locations has kept the price of housing high so that relatively few people in other groups could afford to live in such areas.

Many Whites have particularly sought the seclusion and natural settings of mountain and coastal environments. Because Whites settled first in most such places and demand for these locations remains strong, high percentages of Whites along most of the coast and in the local mountains is to be expected. In Orange County the names of Newport Beach, Laguna Beach, Dana Point, and San Clemente reflect a similar affluence and high percentage White as do Manhattan and Redondo Beaches, Marina del Rey, and a range of beach communities between LAX and Malibu. The same situation occurs in coastal Ventura County in Ventura Harbor and adjacent beaches and the Channel Islands Harbor and Hollywood Beach areas.

Canyon and mountain settings have been similarly attractive and expensive, so that most residents of Silverado and Modjeska Canyons on the western fringe of the Santa Ana Mountains are White, as are most residents of the newer Rancho Santa Margarita. In the southern foothills of the San Gabriel Mountains are similar places like Monrovia and Glendora. There are even places surrounded by mountains: the once-tiny settlement of Acton in the northern foothills of the San Gabriel Mountians, the long-established city of Ojai in Ventura County, and the growing suburban city of Santa Clarita.

Many census tracts in more mountainous areas are large in size because they contain few people. Large areas of the intense green indicating a high White percentage can be misleading to a map reader who might assume that many people live in such areas. For example, north of Pasadena the large green tract is completely within Angeles National Forest and includes Mt. Wilson; it was home to only 177 people in 2000. Similarly, large tracts in the Santa Monica and Santa Ana Mountains, the Sierra Pelona (the western extension of the San Gabriel Mountains), and the Sespe wilderness country of northern Ventura County have only scattered settlements along the edges, often in canyons.

In the newer suburbs closer to major employment centers, the percentage of Whites is also high, reflecting the higher housing prices of such areas. This pattern is evident in southern Orange County, which contrasts sharply with the more ethnically mixed character of older suburbs in northern Orange County. Calabasas, Santa Clarita, and Thousand Oaks are similar, reflecting recent home building and their relative accessibility.

However, the more distant suburbs of Palmdale, Lancaster, Victorville, and most of Riverside and San Bernardino Counties do not have such high percentages of Whites because Blacks and Latinos can better afford these areas. In those areas the lowest percentage Whites is usually found in older sections of towns such as Palmdale, Corona, Perris, Ontario, and San Bernardino.

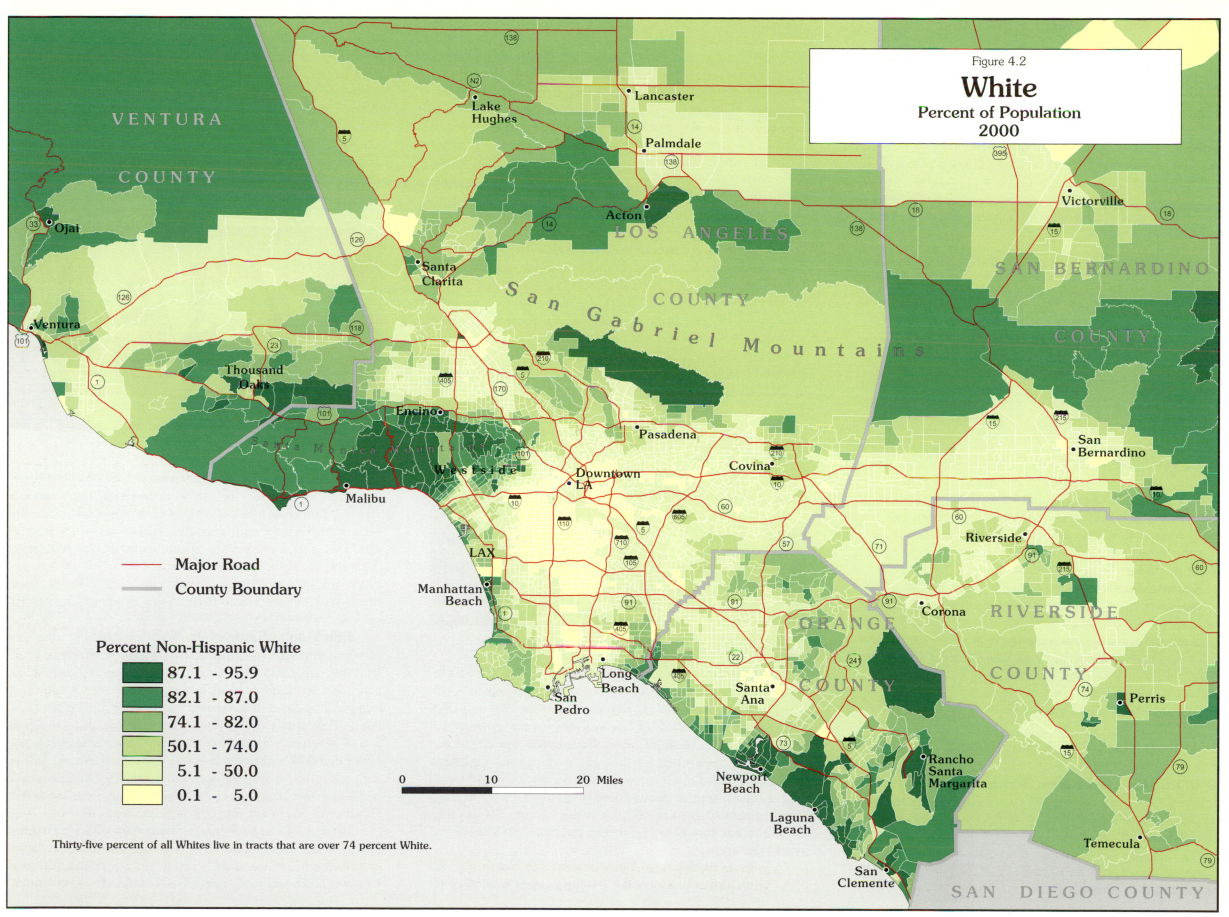

Figure 4.2
White
Percent of Population
2000

Percent Non-Hispanic White

- 87.1 - 95.9
- 82.1 - 87.0
- 74.1 - 82.0
- 50.1 - 74.0
- 5.1 - 50.0
- 0.1 - 5.0

Major Road
County Boundary

0   10   20 Miles

Thirty-five percent of all Whites live in tracts that are over 74 percent White.

White Enclaves and Change

Because Whites have been so dominant numerically until recently and because of the heritage of widespread racist attitudes toward other groups, most Whites have lived in neighborhoods that have not been very ethnically mixed. To describe the change in enclave settlement during the 1990s most thoroughly, we ranked all tracts by their percentage White and report the percentage of Whites residing in tracts of five different percentage-White categories (Table 4.1).

Table 4.1. Enclave Settlement of Whites, 1990 and 2000: Los Angeles CMSA

Percent White in Tracts	Percent Whites in Each Category		Change 1990-2000
	1990	2000	
80 – 100%	35.1	22.3	-12.8
60 – 79%	37.0	36.3	-.7
40 – 59%	17.1	21.0	+3.9
20 – 39%	7.2	14.2	+7.0
0 – 19%	3.6	6.2	+2.6

Sources: 1990 U.S. Census STF1; Census 2000 race tables.

Increased residential mixing of Whites with other groups is clearly evident. The nineties saw a substantial reduction in the percentage of Whites living in tracts that are over 80-percent White and a greater proportion in neighborhoods that were less than 60 percent White. Although this change is significant, the average Southern California White still lives in a neighborhood that is over 60-percent White.

These findings clarify contrasting trends of ethnic residential separation, as measured in a different way elsewhere in this book. Calculations of the index of dissimilarity (Table 7.2) indicate a reduction since 1980 in residential separation between Whites and Blacks but increases in White-Latino and White-Asian residential separation in most counties. It is clear from Table 4.1 that during the 1990s Whites did become more residentially mixed with other groups.

Black Population Change

Black departures from South Central and other enclaves. For over a century the city of Los Angeles has been the main urban center for Blacks in California. For much of this period White segregation of Blacks into restricted areas (sometimes called *ghettoes*) was widespread and legal. The largest such enclave is located in South Central Los Angeles, a large ill-defined area that is mostly south of Interstate 10 and west of Alameda Street. In recent years the area has sometimes been referred to as South Los Angeles.

In the period from the 1920s through 1948, racially restrictive covenants on property deeds were enforceable by the courts of California. These prohibited White homeowners in most areas from selling to Blacks. In more recent decades Whites may have sold or rented to Blacks, but many Whites were often not comfortable with it. Fear of neighborhood invasion by Blacks has motivated many Whites to change neighborhoods. Nevertheless, residential segregation has diminished significantly since about 1970, as is demonstrated in chapter 7.

The number of Blacks living in traditionally segregated neighborhoods continued to diminish during the 1990s. Much of this change has been due to the arrival of Mexican immigrants in search of low-cost housing near job opportunities. Equally important have been the housing needs of new Latino families formed by the U.S.-born sons and daughters of earlier immigrants. Because many Mexican families have pooled their resources among workers and families to pay for housing, they have been able to pay higher rents than many local Blacks or have been able to buy homes. Thus, Latinos have replaced much of the Black population in South Central.

View Park, Baldwin Hills

The demand for more affordable housing produced substantial increases in the prices of single-family houses in South Central during the 1990s. To illustrate, between 1988 and 1999 the lowest-income tracts of Los Angeles County recorded an increase in prices of single-family houses that was 20 percent greater than the average for the county.[2] Single-family houses in tracts over half of whose residents were Black showed a gain of 33 percent in price during those years. Such a tight housing market provided great rewards for South Central homeowners who sold, but it tended to drive up the prices for renters and potential buyers.

Apart from the large historic ghetto of South Central L.A., other former Black enclaves— once called *suburban ghet-*

toes—are evident from some of the larger clusters of blue dots (Figure 4.3). Half a century or more ago when Whites wanted Black families readily available for domestic and other work, many of these old Black enclaves were not far from affluent White areas. Such Black ghettos were found in Pasadena, Monrovia, Long Beach, Santa Ana, Riverside, and San Bernardino. There was also outmigration from Black enclaves that were not as old—Pacoima in the San Fernando Valley, established in the late 1940s, and Pomona, dating from the 1960s. Just as has occurred in South Central, these former ghettoes have become increasingly Latino.

Jazz club, Leimert Park

When Blacks leave smaller traditional enclaves like Santa Ana, the disappearance of recognizable Black neighborhoods makes it difficult to retain a sense of community.[3] This has also occurred in Oxnard, which has long had a small Black population. During the 1990s many Blacks left the area. With their declining numbers and the growing proportion of Latinos, Blacks felt they were losing their community.[4] Many Oxnard Blacks have moved back to their original states in the South.

Black suburbanization. Black movement to the suburbs has been motivated particularly by the intensity of problems they experienced in the central city: gangs and guns, drugs, poor schools, racial profiling, and frequent robberies and other crimes.[5] The dispersal to suburbs began about four decades ago, but until the 1980s the numbers were small, resulting in a feeling of isolation within those mostly White suburbs. By the 1980s and 1990s these shifts were expanding geographically, with many Blacks moving into older suburbs like Lakewood, north and east Long Beach, Bellflower, Paramount, Lawndale, Hawthorne, Mar Vista, and Culver City (Figure 4.3).

In the 1980s and 1990s many Blacks settled somewhat farther away in places like the San Fernando Valley, Santa Clarita, and northern Orange County cities such as Buena Park and Cypress. The residential dispersal of these Blacks is evident.

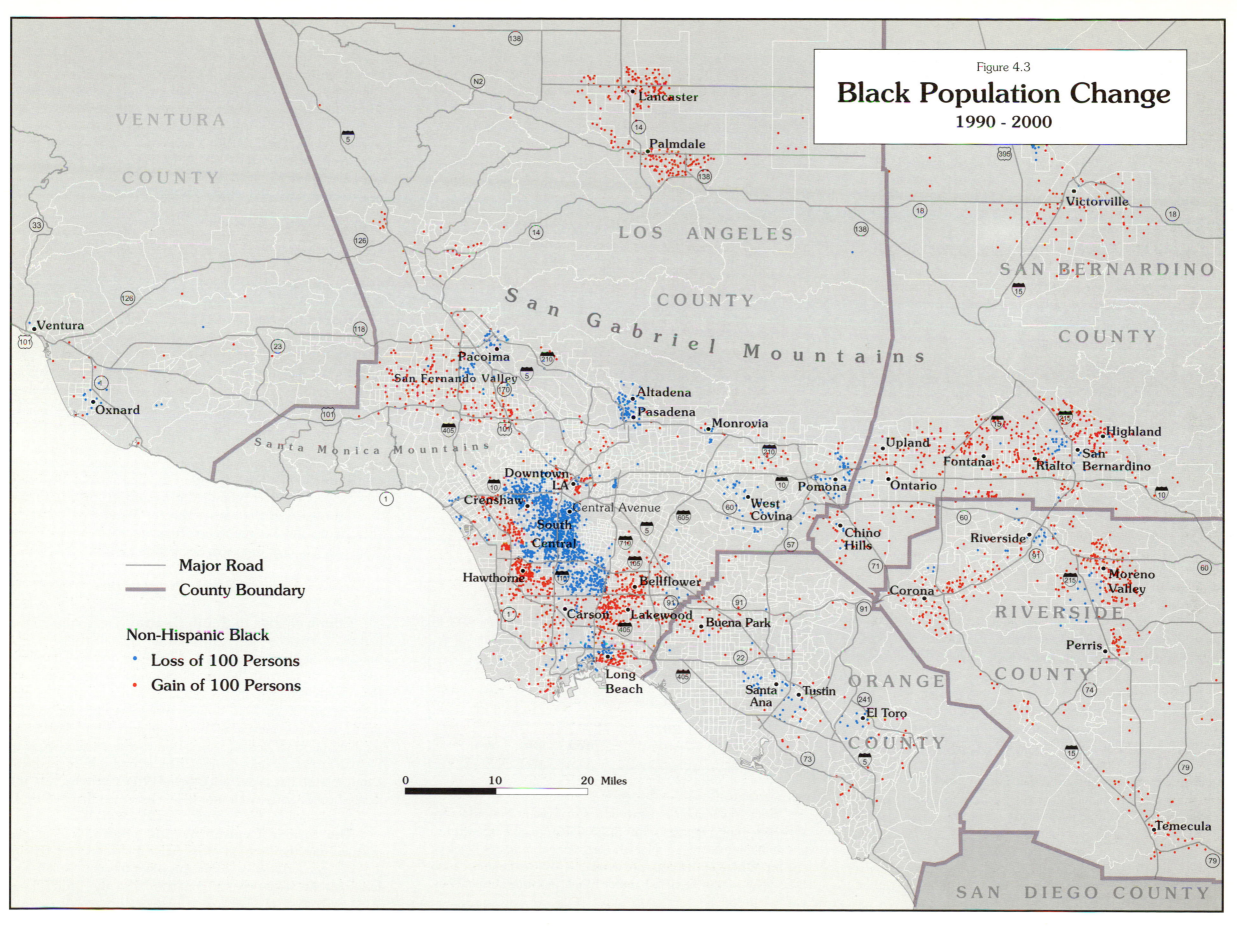

Figure 4.3
Black Population Change
1990 - 2000

Major Road
County Boundary

Non-Hispanic Black
• Loss of 100 Persons
• Gain of 100 Persons

0   10   20 Miles

Other Blacks moved to still more distant destinations, where relatively lower housing prices made homeownership possible for many. These were often the fast-growing cities of Lancaster and Palmdale in the Antelope Valley, the Victorville area, or places in western Riverside and San Bernardino Counties like Upland, Rialto, Fontana, Highland, Corona, Perris, and Moreno Valley. Such places have also been popular with Latinos, so that both Blacks and Latinos have been replacing former White residents in many of these outer suburbs. The main problem with such locations has been the extremely time-consuming commute for those people who continue to work in Los Angeles or Orange County.

Patterns of Black-White Change in Outer Suburbs

During the 1990s both Whites and Blacks continued to settle in what appear to be the more expensive tracts in these outlying suburbs, resulting in little if any residential separation. People can point to these metropolitan-fringe neighborhoods to support the view that Blacks and Whites are coming closer together and that race is becoming less important in America.

On the other hand, in many less affluent neighborhoods the story appears somewhat different. A close comparison of the maps of White change (Figure 4.1) and Black change (Figure 4.3) indicates that these neighborhoods are often becoming more separated racially. Such neighborhoods—in older, more central parts of Rialto, Moreno Valley, Perris, Highland, Hesperia, Lancaster, and Palmdale—experienced net White losses during the 1990s while Blacks, as well as Latinos, moved into the houses vacated by Whites.

Because Black settlement in formerly all-White suburbs and subsequent White flight from Black in-movement has been widespread in the United States since the 1950s, it would not be surprising to find it also in these outer suburbs. However, society in Southern California has changed substantially over the last few decades, and several factors (in addition to possible White flight) are probably involved in explaining a trend toward racial separation in these areas.

Newer outlying suburbs in large metropolitan areas like Los Angeles are good places to examine contemporary residential separation without influences from older residents and settlement patterns. We are unable to analyze here the processes involved in the separation between Whites and Blacks and the similar processes involved in White-Latino residential separation. However, several Black professionals who know the Los Angeles area did comment on factors they thought might be important in explaining this pattern.[6]

Economic factors. Most buyers of homes (regardless of ethnicity) desire a better house as an investment for the future.

However, Blacks and Latinos are less likely to be able to purchase more expensive houses as a result of their lower average incomes and accumulated wealth.[7] It might be thought that Blacks prefer to live in neighborhoods with slightly higher proportions of Blacks. However, it appears that Blacks often prefer the opposite—to live in neighborhoods with higher percentages of Whites. This is because such neighborhoods seem to hold their value better than more mixed areas.

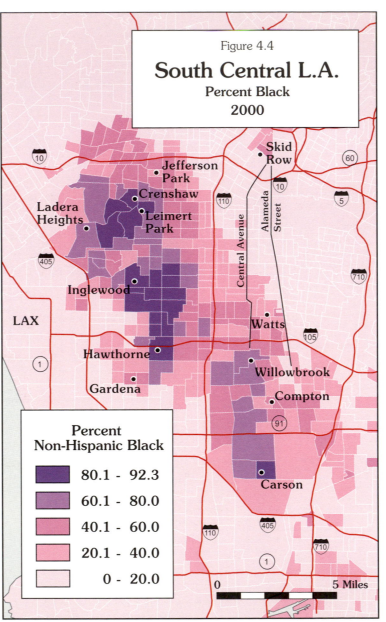

Figure 4.4

South Central L.A.

Percent Black

2000

Percent Non-Hispanic Black

■	80.1 - 92.3
■	60.1 - 80.0
■	40.1 - 60.0
■	20.1 - 40.0
□	0 - 20.0

0   5 Miles

Some outer suburbs contain few apartment buildings and very little rental housing, thus making such neighborhoods less attainable for poorer people, who are more commonly Black or Latino. Where rental units are available, Whites are more likely than Blacks to be able to afford high monthly rents. Thus,

economic factors are important in explaining lower Black percentages in more expensive neighborhoods.

Recommendations. There are also several non-economic factors that may play important roles in neighborhood ethnic differentiation in newer suburbs. One is possible recommendations by friends and perceptions about how a newcomer will be received. Early Black settlers in a neighborhood often recommend it to relatives and friends in a process called chain migration, thus tending to build up Black percentages in certain neighborhoods. For potential apartment renters, a similar recommendation may include the information that the manager of a certain apartment building will rent to Blacks. Also, realtors may make assumptions about the needs and desires of their clients and then subtly steer Black and White clients toward different neighborhoods.

Discrimination and White flight. Discrimination by landlords and apartment building managers may result in lower Black percentages in tracts where renters predominate. For homeowners, discrimination by mortgage lenders appears to limit the ability of Blacks to acquire the housing for which their incomes should qualify them.[8] Lastly, Whites may leave neighborhoods because of growing minority numbers (White flight) or resentment over the lifestyle or activities of newcomers.

Thus, there is no simple explanation for what appears to be increasing Black-White separation in outer metropolitan suburbs.[9] General factors behind ethnic residential separation are also discussed near the end of chapter 7 under the headings "Explaining the Persistence of Residential Separation" and "Explaining Recent Trends in Separation Levels".

Varying Black Proportions

Ethnic change in South Central. The South Central part of Los Angeles has experienced substantial change in ethnic composition in the twentieth century. Although always somewhat mixed with White, Blacks, and Mexicans, it went from mostly White, to mostly Black, to mostly Latino. The first shift occurred from 1920 through 1940, because the original White residents moved to newer suburbs while instituting mechanisms of residential segregation that restricted Blacks to the older parts of South Central. The second shift to predominantly Latino has taken place since 1970, partly because the demand for housing by Latinos has far exceeded that by Blacks.

The former Central Avenue ghetto. It might be assumed that the location of the large Black enclave (Figure 4.4) has remained the same, but this is not the case. A half century ago the largest Black concentration was centered on

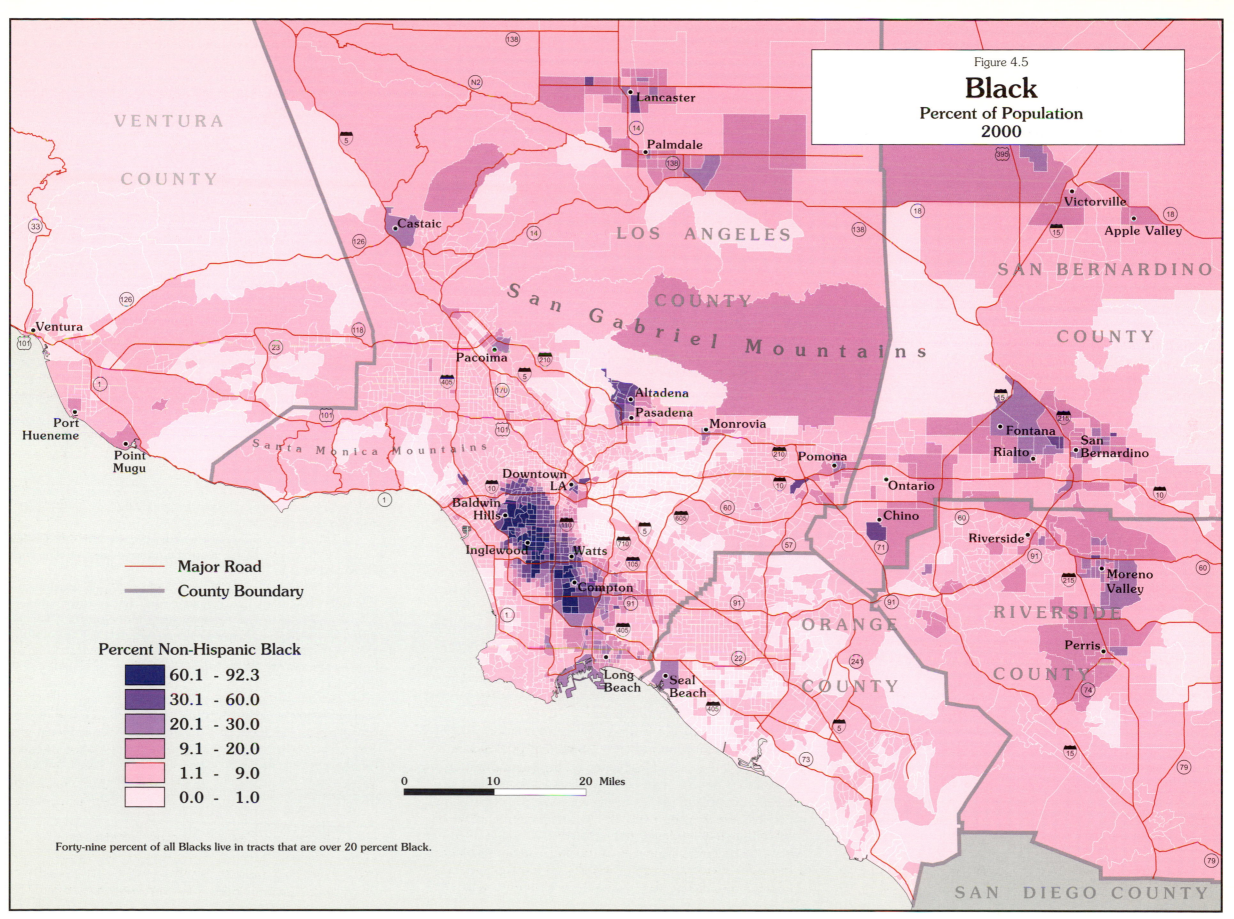

Figure 4.5

Black
Percent of Population
2000

Percent Non-Hispanic Black

- 60.1 - 92.3
- 30.1 - 60.0
- 20.1 - 30.0
- 9.1 - 20.0
- 1.1 - 9.0
- 0.0 - 1.0

— Major Road
— County Boundary

0   10   20 Miles

Forty-nine percent of all Blacks live in tracts that are over 20 percent Black.

Central Avenue near Vernon Avenue—four miles to the east of its present location (Figures 4.3 and 4.5). People lived in single-family houses on numerous side streets, but Central Avenue itself had a range of churches, stores, and professional offices. It was also well known for its jazz clubs, patronized by many Whites as well as Blacks. On the other hand, because of overcrowding and low incomes from restrictions on the jobs Blacks were permitted to hold, that ghetto was probably the poorest section of Los Angeles.

The rigidity of segregation in those days was evident in the low percentages of Blacks in surrounding cities. As of 1960, Compton, which would soon become predominantly Black, had only 154 Blacks, representing only a fifth of one percent of the city's population.[10] To the west, the cities of Gardena, Hawthorne, and Inglewood together had a total population of 132,000 but only 40 Blacks. To the east, Alameda Street constituted a sharp racial divide (Figure 4.4). In 1960 the major cities east of Alameda Street—Huntington Park, Maywood, South Gate, Lynwood, Bell, and Bell Gardens—had only 44 Black residents out of a population totaling over 162,000.

Out-movement and westward shift. In the 1960s, as the social and legal structures that had supported segregation began to crumble, Blacks moved in large numbers westward and southward. White flight from advancing Black settlement opened up opportunities to rent or buy better homes. In the late 1960s many headed southward, to Compton and beyond, to the new city of Carson. The movement into Carson has continued; in 2000 a tract in Carson near California State University, Dominguez Hills, was over 80 percent Black (Figure 4.4).

More middle- and upper-class Blacks moved westward, often into the Baldwin Hills. In the 1990s the Baldwin Hills area, including the Crenshaw district and Leimert Park, became the geographical focus of Los Angeles' Black community in the northern portion of the relocated Black enclave.

Despite the predominant out-movement of Blacks from South Central, there are advantages to living in or near a geographically concentrated ethnic community. Black residents are often more comfortable living in mostly Black neighborhoods, a large enclave can be a political power base, and it is easier to raise children with a stronger sense of their ethnic heritage. Ethnically oriented stores and services, entertainment, churches, and other institutions are nearby. Thus, some middle- and upper-class Blacks who could have left South Central have remained, and others have sometimes returned after having lived in predominantly White suburbs. As of 2000, 40 percent of Black households in South Central owned their own home, a rate higher than that for Blacks in Los Angeles County as a whole.[11]

Other areas. The mostly middle-class, racially mixed Black enclave in rustic Altadena in the foothills continues to be important. However, enclaves (Monrovia, Pacoima, Long Beach, Pomona, and San Bernardino) in poorer areas on flat lands have been much diminished as Latinos have been arriving and Blacks dispersing since 1970. The former enclaves in Santa Ana and Oxnard are no longer visible on Figure 4.5.

Because Black men have been incarcerated at higher rates than their percentage in the general population, tracts containing prisons occasionally stand out on maps (Figure 4.5). In Chino's California Institution for Men, Black men represent over 30 percent of the inmates in that state prison. A similar situation is evident west of Lancaster, at the Mira Loma Detention Facility and state prison, and in Castaic, at Los Angeles County's Peter Pitchess Detention Center.

Military installations have usually had higher percentages of Blacks as a result of earlier desegregation of the military and greater opportunities for advancement without regard to color. Although the Air Force bases in Riverside and San Bernardino Counties have closed, this pattern is evident at the Navy's weapons storage facility in Seal Beach in northern Orange County. Similarly, naval installations in Ventura County—the Seabee base at Port Hueneme and the missile test facility at Point Mugu—have higher percentages of Blacks than any other tracts in that county.

Black Enclaves and Changes

Since the days of rigid racial segregation in the 1960s, Blacks in Southern California have been leaving their enclaves. However, the Black enclave in South Central remains culturally, socially, and politically, important, despite a shift from its original focus on the Central Avenue to the Leimert Park area.

Nevertheless, the importance of Black enclaves in the residential distribution has diminished in recent decades. The trend is particularly evident during the 1990s (Table 4.2). Although 45 percent of Blacks in 2000 lived in tracts that are enclaves as we have defined them, the 11 percent reduction in enclave settlement during the 1990s represents a substantial increase in Black residential mixing.

The decline of Black residential concentration parallels the continued reduction in Black-White residential separation as measured and discussed in chapter 7. The deconcentration of Blacks results directly from both residential dispersal and slow population growth in the leading county, Los Angeles County, which has experienced net Black out-migration since about 1980. Ultimately, however, the reduced importance of Black enclaves reflects the same shifts in racial attitudes and broad

cultural and economic changes in American society that have made possible a large Black middle class in Southern California and in much of metropolitan America.

Table 4.2. Enclave Settlement of Blacks, 1990 and 2000: Los Angeles CMSA

Threshold for Enclaves		Percent Blacks in Enclaves		Change 1990-2000
1990	2000	1990	2000	
23.9	22.8	55.9	44.8	-11.1

Notes: Within the total population of the five counties Blacks constituted 7.95% in 1990 and 7.60% in 2000. All census tracts in which Blacks are represented at more than three times these percentages are considered ethnic residential enclaves, as explained in chapter 1. Threshold values are the lowest percentage values that define enclave settlement for any group and year. Thresholds and percentages include fractionally assigned mixed-race Blacks.

Notes

1. For details on these ethnic communities, see Allen and Turner (1997).

2. Craine (2000), 42.

3. Yi (2001).

4. Kelley (2001).

5. De Graaf (2001), 419, 431-433.

6. We thank Joseph Holloway, Eugene Grigsby, Herman De Bose, and Sharon Kinlaw for their thoughts, which we have incorporated into our interpretation.

7. The disparity in average wealth between White and Black households is much greater than the average income difference (Oliver and Shapiro 1995).

8. Reibel (2000); Aldana and Dymski (2001). Related to discrimination is the fact that potential Black homeowners are more likely than Whites to look for home loans in the subprime lending market, where they are charged higher interest rates and occasionally predatory fees by lenders (Stein and Libby 2001). Such practices have the effect of restricting Black prospective homeowners to lower-priced homes than Whites.

9. A major research project in the early 1990s (the Multi-City Study) attempted to unravel the various factors behind residential segregation in Los Angeles County and in greater Atlanta, Boston, and Detroit. The results—for the older parts of metropolitan areas rather than the outer suburbs—were expectedly complex except that racial attitudes, economic considerations, and discrimination were the most important (Charles 2001; Wilson and Hammer 2001).

10. U.S. Bureau of the Census (1963), Table 21.

11. Myers (2002).

5. Latinos and American Indians

The relative status and power of Whites, Indians, and Latinos and the ethnic relations between them are based partly on the heritage of the past. During the last century Whites have clearly had the advantage while Mexicans (easily the largest Latino group) and Indians were relegated to a much lower position in a racialized social structure. The social differentiation between Whites and both Mexicans and Indians is weaker than in the past, but ethnic differences and tensions do continue, although prejudices and stereotypes are rarely mentioned in public.

White-Mexican differences have been exacerbated by the arrival over the last three decades of large numbers of poor Mexican immigrants with little formal education. These, in turn, have faced a growing average income gap between Whites and Mexicans.[1]

Largest U.S. Latino population. Latinos in Southern California outnumber Latinos in the other leading CMSA concentrations—New York, Chicago, Miami, and Houston—combined. Southern California is clearly the preeminent Latino center of the United States.

Los Angeles County is easily the most important place in the United States for people whose heritage is Mexican and Central American. In fact, Los Angeles County has three times more people of Mexican origin than the next largest primary metropolitan area (Chicago) and three times more people of Central American origin than the second largest such metro area (Washington, DC). For Latinos of South American origin, Los Angeles County is the third most important center, following New York and Miami.

Although Southern California is home to more Latinos than any other metropolitan area, during the 1990s Mexican immigrants became less likely to settle in Southern California than in the remainder of the United States.[2] This suggests that in the future Southern California will become a less dominant Latino center.

Table 5.1 Latino (Hispanic) Populations, 1990 and 2000: Counties in Los Angeles CMSA

Los Angeles CMSA

	Census 1990	Census 2000	Estimate 2000	Pct. Chg. 1990-00
Latino	4,779,178	6,598,488	6,598,488	38.1
Mexican	3,751,278	4,962,046	5,313,727	41.7
Central American	503,400	436,742	644,316	28.0

Los Angeles County

	Census 1990	Census 2000	Estimate 2000	Pct. Chg. 1990-00
Latino	3,345,273	4,242,213	4,242,213	26.8
Mexican	2,527,160	3,041,974	3,257,572	28.9
Central American	453,048	372,777	549,950	21.4

Orange County

	Census 1990	Census 2000	Estimate 2000	Pct. Chg. 1990-00
Latino	564,828	875,579	875,579	55.0
Mexican	474,818	712,496	762,994	60.7
Central American	25,438	27,648	40,788	60.3

Riverside County

	Census 1990	Census 2000	Estimate 2000	Pct. Chg. 1990-00
Latino	307,514	559,575	559,575	82.0
Mexican	270,098	463,465	496,312	83.8
Central American	8,398	11,895	17,548	109.0

San Bernardino County

	Census 1990	Census 2000	Estimate 2000	Pct. Chg. 1990-00
Latino	378,582	669,387	669,387	76.7
Mexican	321,572	532,186	569,904	77.2
Central American	12,452	19,735	29,115	133.8

Ventura County

	Census 1990	Census 2000	Estimate 2000	Pct. Chg. 1990-00
Latino	176,952	251,734	251,734	42.3
Mexican	157,630	211,925	226,945	44.0
Central American	4,064	4,687	6,915	70.4

Patterns of Latino Population Growth

Southern California's Latino population grew by over a third during the 1990s to a total of about 6.6 million (Table 5.1). As of 2000, there were about 50,000 more Latinos than Whites in Southern California. In Los Angeles County, Latinos began outnumbering Whites about 1993.

The rapid growth rate of Latinos in California during the 1990s was more the result of natural increase than net migration. The birthrate among Latinos, particularly high among immigrants from Mexico, combined with a low death rate to explain two-thirds or more of Latino increase during the 1990s in Southern California.[3]

Due to data problems with the Census 2000 counts of specific Hispanic nationalities, the Southern California totals for Mexicans and Central Americans as estimated by the Pew Hispanic Center (Table 5.1) are probably superior to the Census 2000 figures.[4] We derived county estimates from the Pew estimates, and we recommend our estimates as better county totals of Mexicans and Central Americans than the numbers provided by Census 2000.

The Pew estimates for 2000 indicate that 80 percent of all Hispanics in the five-county Los Angeles CMSA are Mexicans. The next largest Hispanic nationalities and their estimated totals are Salvadorans (340,229) and Guatemalans (186,496).

Latino numbers increased least in Los Angeles County and most in the four outlying counties. The highest rates of Latino growth were in Riverside and San Bernardino Counties, the

Table 5.1 Sources: Data for 1990: U.S. Census Bureau 1993a, Table 5; 1993c, Table 6. Data for 2000: U.S. Census Bureau: http://www.census.gov; Suro (2002), Table 11.

Notes: Estimates for the Los Angeles CMSA are by the Pew Hispanic Center, as explained in chapter 2, "Changes in Census Procedures, Hispanic or Latino nationalities." Estimates for counties are our apportioning of the Pew estimates to each county based on each group's distribution according to Census 2000. Percent change 1990-2000 shows the rate of increase between the 1990 census and that 2000 estimate.

leading destinations for people looking for newer homes priced lower than in Los Angeles County. Central Americans were particularly likely to move to these same two counties, as well as to Ventura County.

Growth of existing barrios (enclaves). On the map of Latino change the densest clusters represent the growth of Latino ethnic concentrations (Figure 5.1). These develop both from continued Latino replacement of non-Latino residents in neighborhoods that are already partially Latino, and from geographical expansion of already existing Latino neighborhoods into adjacent areas.

The larger areas of intense Latino growth have low- or moderate-priced housing, either near city centers, in or near industrial areas, or in older suburbs. In some cases Latino families pool their finances to buy moderate-priced suburban homes rather than continue to pay rent.

The largest expanding barrio or enclave is south of Downtown L.A., roughly the area from the Harbor Freeway (Interstate 110) to the San Gabriel River Freeway (Interstate 605), including South Central L.A., Huntington Park, South Gate, Paramount, Downey, Norwalk, and Whittier. Most of this area is over 80 percent Latino, and some tracts are over 95 percent Latino. In some places the edge of this growing Latino enclave is sharply defined by industrial land use. Thus, there is little Latino growth in Vernon and the City of Commerce, Santa Fe Springs, and Carson although many Latinos are employed in manufacturing and other jobs in these places.

Similar patterns of growth occurred in the San Fernando Valley, where jobs in older industries are generally in the older eastern portion of the Valley. The large Mexican settlement in the East Valley, which originated over a century ago in the small city of San Fernando, expanded in all directions, as did the Canoga Park barrio in the West Valley. Throughout the Valley, in areas of low- and moderate-priced housing, Latinos moved into the homes and apartments of departing Whites.

Dispersal to more distant suburbs. Latino numbers have been growing rapidly in the outlying suburbs. In most cases this represents movement into housing vacated by Whites. This process has been occurring for two or three decades in central cities and older suburbs closer to Los Angeles, but during the 1990s it also characterized cities more peripheral to the metropolitan area.

Eastern and southeastern Los Angeles County may contain the most important concentration of successful, middle-class Mexican Americans in Southern California and, possibly, the United States. These families live in the suburban cities of Whittier, Downey, Hacienda Heights, Covina, West Covina, and nearby places.

The shift in ethnic composition from White to Latino is clearly evident in more distant suburbs (Figures 5.1 and 4.1). The factors involved in the details of White-Latino residential separation are covered in the section on "Patterns of Black-White Change in Outer Suburbs" in chapter 4.

Some Latinos have also settled in the more expensive, mostly White residential developments in outer suburbs. These are exemplified by the Orange County cities of Mission Viejo, Laguna Hills, and San Juan Capistrano. A similar pattern is found in the many developments between Corona and Temecula in Riverside County.

Latino settlement in more distant suburbs symbolizes the upward mobility of the mostly U.S.-born Latinos.[5] It represent significant economic success, particularly for those who become homeowners in the process of moving.

Areas of Latino Decline

Because Latino population growth has been so widespread, areas that experienced decline give indications of some less typical dynamics of ethnic neighborhood change. Latino numbers declined in certain places for four basic reasons: loss of low- or moderate-priced housing because of urban redevelopment, reduced crowding, the replacement of Latinos by other ethnic groups, and the closure of key military facilities.

Loss of housing. In the process of urban land-use change, housing is often eliminated, resulting in a decline of neighborhood population. Older apartment buildings or houses, many of whose tenants are Latino, are often replaced with shopping centers, office buildings, or newer and more expensive apartments or condos.

This has occurred in a zone around L.A.'s Downtown and near the coast in the Venice area. To the west of the Harbor Freeway (Interstate 110) and south of Downtown near Staples Center, buildings have been demolished or condemned for construction of office buildings and upscale apartment buildings. Other housing nearby was lost for construction of the Belmont Learning Complex. In Venice, a popular area with rising housing prices, many older apartment buildings have been remodeled to create larger apartments that can then command much higher rents.[6] Such gentrification has displaced many Latinos and has resulted has resulted in a net loss of housing units. Similarly, in parts of Hollywood, Latino declines are probably explained by the renovation and upgrading of apartment buildings to be rented at higher prices, although there may also have been a net loss of apartment units in some neighborhoods.

A loss of older housing also occurred east of Downtown, in the "flats" between the Los Angeles River and Boyle Heights.

In the late 1990s most residents of three large old public housing projects (Aliso Village, Pico Gardens, and Aliso Apartments) had to move elsewhere in anticipation of building demolition and planned rebuilding in more modern and attractive designs.[7] Thus, Census 2000 showed major population losses in these tracts. As of early 2002, some low-income residents were moving into the completely new Pico Aliso and Pico Gardens complexes. In Boyle Heights itself, the 1990s saw some housing demolition on various parcels, some of which occurred as land was cleared for a planned station for the projected extension of the Red Line subway.

Reduced crowding in some neighborhoods. Housing in Boyle Heights and Pico-Union, typically extremely crowded in 1990, became slightly less so during the 1990s. In five Boyle Heights tracts the population declined by an average of 11 percent compared to a one-percent average decline in housing units. Two tracts in Pico-Union averaged an 11-percent drop in population during the nineties but a 14-percent increase in housing units. Another indication of the lower level of crowding is that the average vacancy rate in those seven tracts was 8 percent in 2000 compared to 5 percent in 1990.[8] Strongly Latino East Los Angeles also recorded a small decline (1.7 percent) in population during the 1990s.

The reduction in crowding in such low-rent areas resulted from a mix of influences affecting the relative supply and demand of low-cost housing, but one probable factor was the tendency in the 1990s for Mexican immigrants to settle in places other than Southern California.[9]

Asian and Armenian in-movement. In Monterey Park, the East San Gabriel Valley, and Cerritos, residents who were Latino departed and were, in most cases, replaced by Asians, often Chinese. These localities have become increasingly attractive for Asian immigrants over the last twenty years, and many resident Latinos cashed in their equity in these areas so strongly favored by Asians. Latinos who had been living in apartments may have chosen to leave, but others may have seen rental prices increase or been otherwise pressured to leave by new Asian immigrant landlords and building managers, who preferred renting to members of their own ethnic group.[10]

Hacienda Heights, Walnut, Diamond Bar, and Cerritos are upper-income suburbs composed mostly of modern single-family, detached houses. Asians have been especially eager to live in these areas. Whenever a Latino, Black, or White family leaves these places, it is usually an Asian family that moves in. In nearby parts of San Bernardino County, the small net out-movement of Latinos from some upscale, newly developed neighborhoods in Chino Hills near the Los Angeles County line may reflect the same process of Latino-Asian transfer.

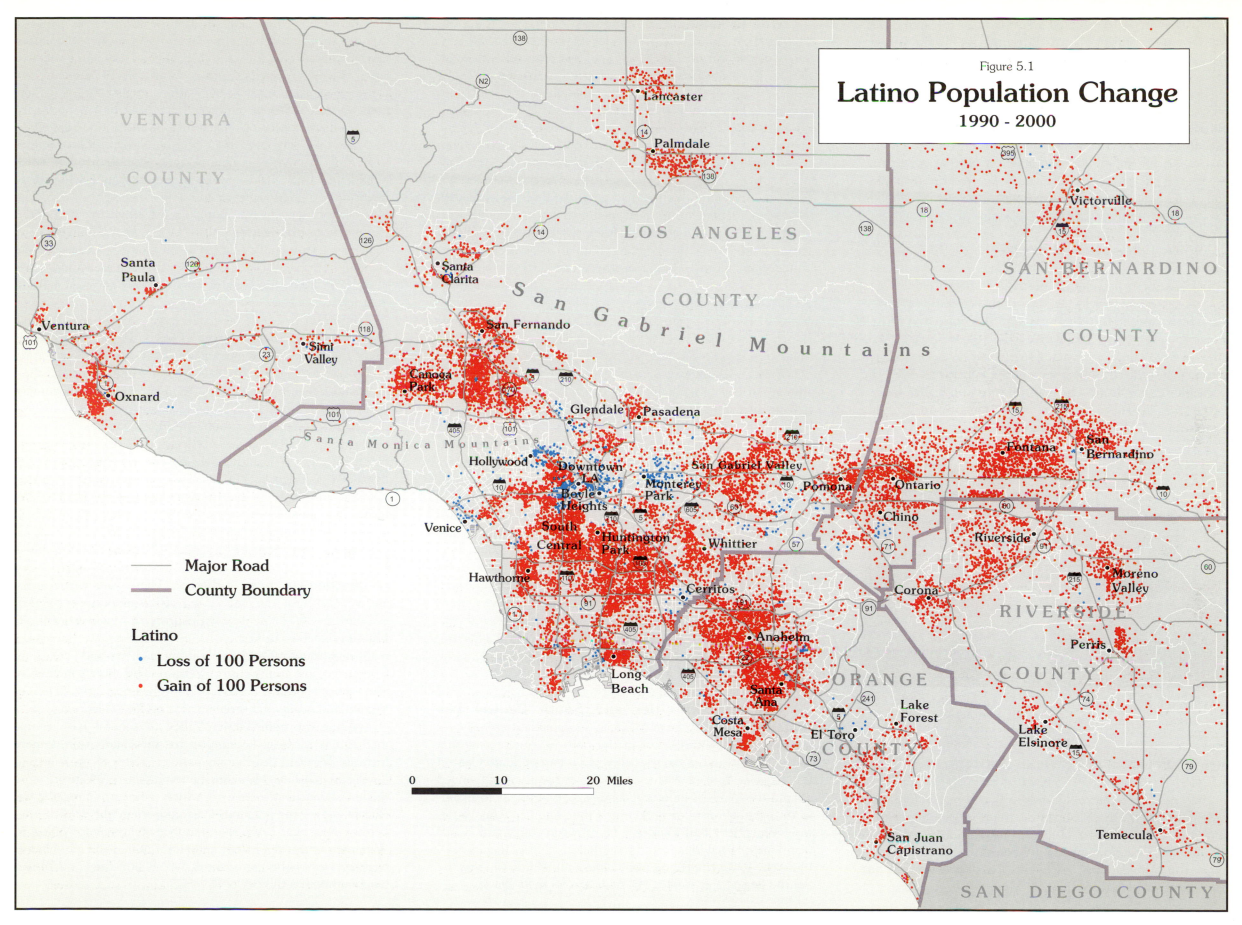

Figure 5.1
Latino Population Change
1990 - 2000

Major Road
County Boundary

Latino
• Loss of 100 Persons
• Gain of 100 Persons

0   10   20 Miles

Latinos also left neighborhoods in west and south Glendale, where they were most likely replaced by Armenians. Glendale represents an unusually strong ethnic enclave that is attractive for Armenians. Many older Armenians, in particular, immigrated from Iran, Lebanon, Armenia, Russia, or other countries and wish to continue their lives in an American Armenian context. As with Latino departures from Monterey Park and Cerritos, this ethnic shift in Glendale probably involved some combination of housing price increases beyond the reach of the Latino renters, good opportunities for Latino homeowners to sell to eager Armenian buyers, and landlord preferences for renting to Armenians.

Military closures and prisons. Latino declines also occurred where major military installations were closed during the 1990s. Military and civilian personnel formerly employed at the bases often had to relocate. The three facilities that are no longer active are El Toro Marine Corps Air Station in central Orange County, March Air Force Base just west of Moreno Valley in Riverside County, and George Air Force Base northwest of Victorville in San Bernardino County. However, the noticeable Latino decline in one tract in Chino represents a drop in the number incarcerated in the state prison, officially known as the California Institution for Men.

Mariachi Plaza, Boyle Heights

Patterns of Mexican Settlement

Because 80 percent of Latinos in Southern California are of Mexican origin, the Mexican distribution determines most features of the Latino or Hispanic distribution.[11] Although there is some residential mixing of Mexicans with other Latino groups, the features most evident in the distribution are the areas which are over three-quarters Mexican (Figure 5.2).

The Eastside of Los Angeles. During the twentieth century the area east of Los Angeles' Downtown and the L.A. River developed into a very large and intensely Mexican enclave or barrio. Sometimes this entire Eastside area is called East Los Angeles (Figure 5.2), but politically it is divided into two parts. The portion that is closer to L.A.'s Downtown and the river is called Boyle Heights; it is part of Los Angeles City. To the east lies East Los Angeles, which is unincorporated county territory (Figure 5.3).

In the 1890s Boyle Heights was a new suburb of Los Angeles, but during the next half century it became an important reception area for newly arrived migrants and immigrants. From the 1920s through the 1940s it was strongly Jewish but Japanese, Mexicans, Russians, and Armenians were well represented. More recently, Jews and others tended to move to other parts of Los Angeles or to newer suburbs. Their former residences were typically occupied by Mexicans—either immigrants or the U.S.-born children and grandchildren of immigrants. Immigration from Mexico since about 1970 has meant that Boyle Heights has become more homogeneously Mexican.

East Los Angeles was built up somewhat later, especially after the street railway arrived in the neighborhood known as Belvedere in the 1920s. Mexicans began to construct homes here, where less restrictive regulations made it easier to build than in Los Angeles City.[12] With a commercial section focused along Whittier Blvd. and continued population growth, Mexican settlement in East Los Angeles has coalesced with Boyle Heights into a very large barrio.

Cities to the east like El Monte and Pico Rivera are also suburbs, but not as old. Because so many Whites have left Los Angeles County since 1960 and because the predominant direction of Mexican suburbanization over the last half century has been eastward, the high percentages of Mexicans found in these two cities and others is not surprising. The movement of Mexican families to homes in newer suburbs has continued to the east in the San Gabriel Valley, to Baldwin Park, La Puente, and other cities, and to the southeast, to La Mirada, Santa Fe Springs, Norwalk, and Whittier.

Southeastern cities and South Central Los Angeles. This very large Mexican settlement stretches over several municipalities. Most of the portion west of Alameda Street lies within Los Angeles City and is part of South Central Los Angeles. East of Alameda Street are seven cities founded around the 1920s as industrial suburbs, containing both manufacturing and homes for workers and their families. These cities (including Bell, Bell Gardens, Huntington Park, and South Gate) are referred to here as the southeastern cities (Figure 5.3). Until the 1960s these cities were almost all White, whereas the South Central area west of Alameda was strongly Black.

In more recent decades most of the Whites who had been living in the southeastern cities have moved away or died, partly in response to the loss of high-paying factory jobs associated with economic restructuring. Some Blacks moved into Lynwood and South Gate, but Latinos, especially immigrants from Mexico and their children, have been by far the largest group of newcomers replacing Whites in these industrial cities.

The relatively low cost of housing is one of its attractions to recent immigrants. Schools and homes are crowded. Immigrants with little education and no understanding of English are trying to survive and adjust as best they can. The older commercial district along Pacific Blvd. in Huntington Park has been strikingly revitalized by the great number of newcomers, and stores have adapted to their new Spanish-speaking clientele. On weekends the thousands of families and other shoppers make Pacific Blvd. busier than most enclosed malls in Southern California.

Mexicans have also moved in large numbers into the area west of Alameda Street (in South Central Los Angeles), occupying the homes left by departing Blacks. A third of Latino households in South Central Los Angeles in 2000 owned their own homes—an increase since 1990 and perhaps a reflection of lower housing prices in that area.[13]

In 2000, Mexicans outnumbered Blacks in nearly all tracts between the Harbor Freeway (Interstate 110) and Alameda Street that lie north of the Century Freeway (Interstate 105). Even Watts, long symbolic of Black poverty in Los Angeles, now has more Latinos than Blacks (Figure 5.3). Thus, in the forty years since 1960 areas east of Alameda changed from almost all White to almost all Latino and those west of Alameda changed from being strongly Black to mostly Latino.

Settlement near industry. These very large barrios are not far from the largest industrial area in central Los Angeles, in which Mexicans constitute the main work force. Industry is focused in Vernon, a city which has few residents but many manufacturing and warehousing facilities, and in the City Commerce, just to the east of Vernon. The short commute of Latinos from both the Eastside and southeastern cities to jobs in Vernon and nearby industrial areas is evident (Figure 5.3).

While the San Gabriel Valley in general has become increasingly Mexican because of this suburbanization, a more intricate Mexican distribution pattern relates to proximity to lower-cost housing. Mexicans have tended to locate in more modest, older suburbs, many of which are near industrial cities (Figure 5.2). This is found, for example, in the Hawthorne-Lennox area near LAX, the eastern San Fernando Valley, in Wilmington near the harbor and oil refineries, the more industrial sections of the San Gabriel Valley, and the Casa Blanca neighborhood in the city of Riverside.

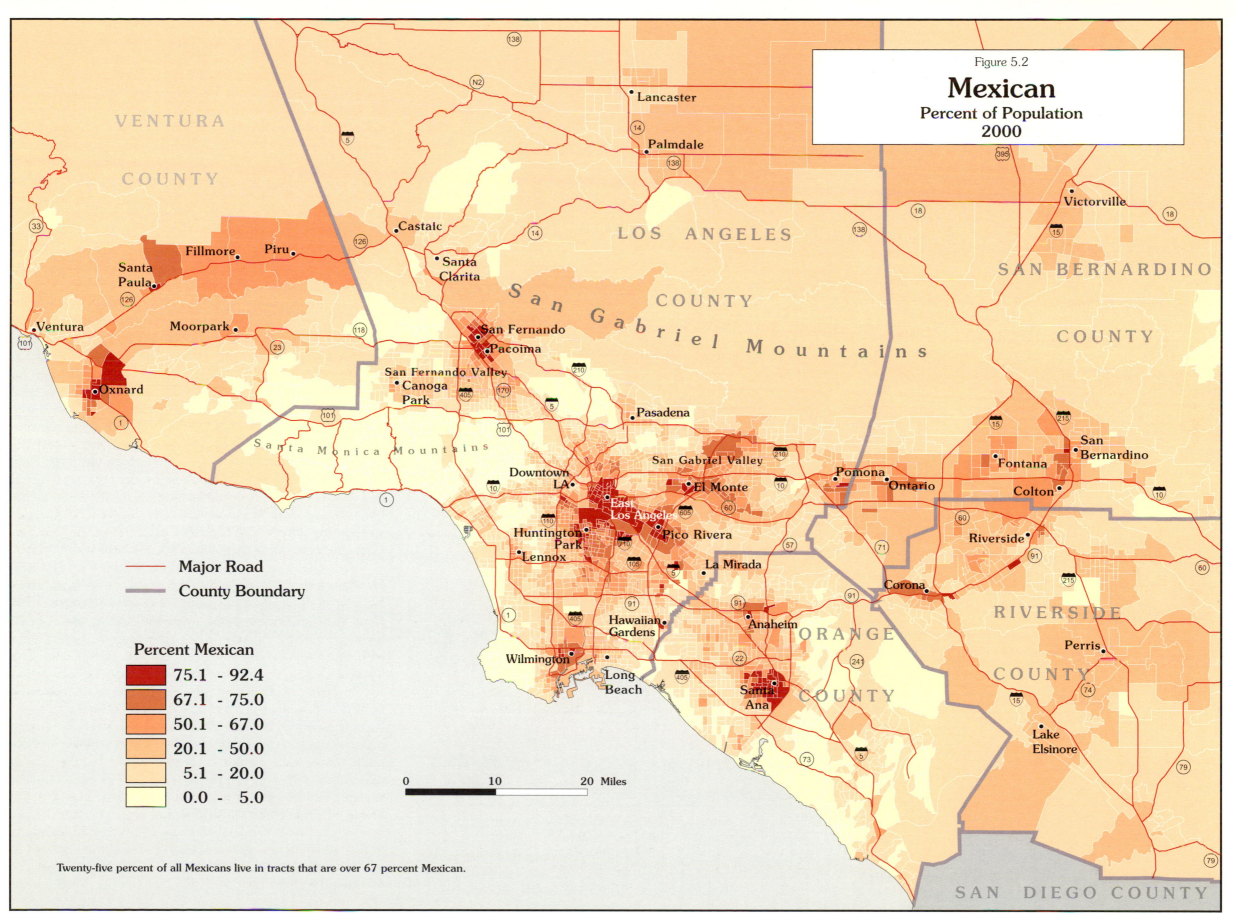

Figure 5.2

Mexican
Percent of Population
2000

Percent Mexican
- 75.1 - 92.4
- 67.1 - 75.0
- 50.1 - 67.0
- 20.1 - 50.0
- 5.1 - 20.0
- 0.0 - 5.0

Major Road
County Boundary

Twenty-five percent of all Mexicans live in tracts that are over 67 percent Mexican.

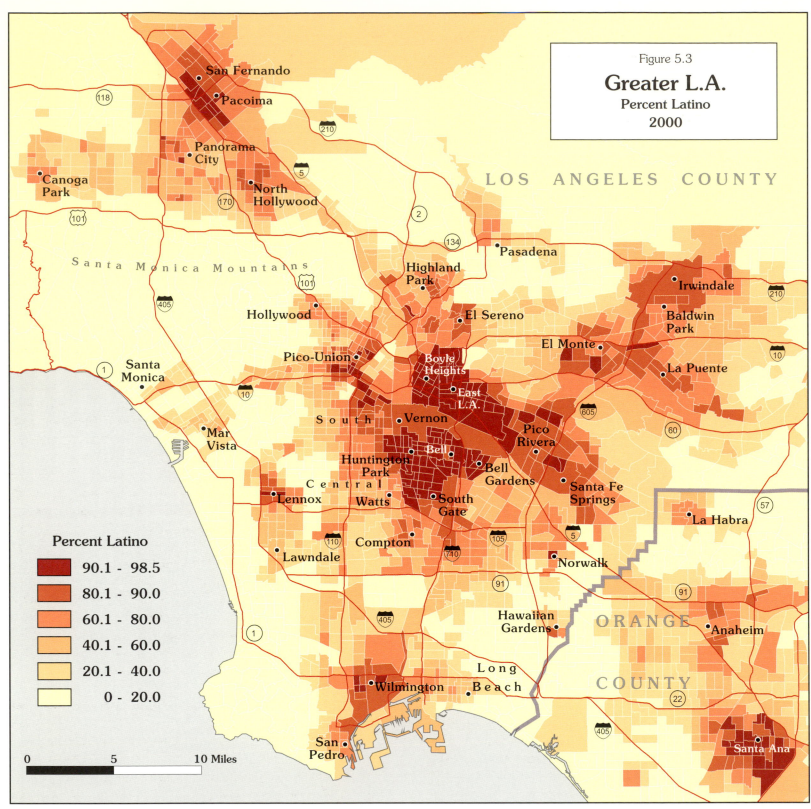

Figure 5.3

Greater L.A.
Percent Latino
2000

Percent Latino

	90.1 - 98.5
	80.1 - 90.0
	60.1 - 80.0
	40.1 - 60.0
	20.1 - 40.0
	0 - 20.0

0   5   10 Miles

and 2000 over 75-percent of the residents of the tract closest to the yards had Spanish surnames or were Mexican.

Urban barrios with farm-worker origins. Many barrios first appeared about a century ago as villages or *colonias* for Mexican farm workers and their families. During the last half of the twentieth century most houses in the *colonias* were completely rebuilt or substantially improved, and the agricultural landscape that once surrounded the villages was transformed as shopping centers and thousands of new suburban homes were built. The *colonias* became barrios embedded in an urban landscape. During this same period, these ethnic enclaves expanded geographically as the Mexican population grew but they remained in essentially the same locations. This was the case in the three largest Mexican enclaves outside the central locations discussed earlier (Figure 5.2).

One such enclave is in the east San Fernando Valley, where the original *colonia* was centered in the small city of San Fernando. Although there was a Spanish mission in this area, commercial agriculture with its labor needs best explains the location of the Mexican settlement here.[14] The arrival of the railroad in the mid-1870s stimulated farm and orchard development using local underground water supplies, and agriculture expanded again after 1913, when Sierra Nevada water began to be imported via the Los Angeles Aqueduct. By 1913 Mexicans were doing most of the farm work in Southern California, and in this area they grew and harvested a variety of field crops, as well as olives and oranges and lemons. Mexican women were a leading component of the workforce in the nearby canneries and packing houses. The Canoga Park barrio in the west San Fernando Valley also began as a *colonia* for sugar beet workers.

As agriculture diminished after World War II, local Mexicans shifted to more urban occupations, usually in manufacturing or other blue-collar positions. New generations of resident Mexican families plus new arrivals from Mexico, often friends and relatives, have led to the continued growth and areal expansion of the Mexican enclave in the east San Fernando Valley.

In 1898 the American Sugar Beet Company developed a large new operation on the rich flatlands near the coast of Ventura County.[15] Surrounding the imposing beet-processing plant were sugar beet fields, housing for the workers, and the beginnings of a town—named Oxnard in honor of the head of the company. This entire operation employed several hundred workers, mostly Japanese and Chinese at first, but by 1920, mostly Mexicans, many of whom had been recruited by the company. Most workers and their families lived in a *colonia* next to the railroad tracks and somewhat separated from the rest of residential Oxnard.[16] By 1960 Mexicans constituted 21 percent of Oxnard's population, but over half of the Mexicans in

A few Mexican settlements near industrial areas were originally begun as homes for railroad workers. To illustrate, census tracts near railroad yards in Colton and San Bernardino have long been strongly Mexican. In Colton—an important route junction point and switching yard for the Southern Pacific Railroad (now part of the Union Pacific)—the tract that contains the railroad yards and older, small houses lies on the south side of Interstate 10. In 1970 over 90 percent of that tract's residents had Spanish surnames although in 2000 only two-thirds of the residents were Mexican. In San Bernardino, in both 1970

Oxnard were beyond the bounds of the small, poor area of *la colonia*. With Mexican population growth since that time and some continued dispersal, a large area in Oxnard and vicinity is over 75-percent Mexican (Figure 5.2).

Farming has remained very important in the Oxnard area although sugar beets faded long ago and have been replaced by strawberries and a range of vegetables. Farm work is still a source of employment for Mexicans here compared to the more urbanized San Fernando Valley, but most Mexicans are employed in service-sector or manufacturing jobs.

A few miles to the northeast, the Santa Clarita Valley (adjacent to Route 126) is another agricultural area, best known for its lemon production, that is over half Mexican (Figure 5.2). Although Mexican settlement in the small Valley towns of Santa Paula, Fillmore, and Piru originated with farm work, in 1990 only 21 percent of Latinos in Santa Paula and Fillmore worked mainly in agriculture.[17] Many Mexicans and Whites who work in Ventura or Santa Clarita have moved to the small towns of Santa Paula, Fillmore, and Piru.

A similar process occurred in Orange County. The many smaller barrios in the northern part of that county originated as approximately a dozen separate *colonias*.[18] These housed the families that worked in the orange groves and packing houses that gave the county its name. The very large Mexican barrio in Santa Ana formed from the growth and coalescing of three former farm-worker *colonias*.

Reasons for continuity of traditional barrios. The striking geographical stability of farm-worker and near-industry Mexican enclaves over many decades is due primarily to two key factors: (1) the continued demand for low-cost housing on the part of poor Mexicans and (2) the absence of any large group with such limited financial resources that it, too, must seek out the cheapest housing available.

Central Americans

Central Americans include those people of Hispanic origin who listed Salvadoran, Guatemalan, Honduran, Costa Rican, and Panamanian ancestries. In Southern California the largest Central American nationalities are Salvadoran and Guatemalan, and the influence of these nationalities dominates the distribution of Central Americans.

There has been concern over less-than-expected totals of specific Hispanic nationalities such as Salvadoran and Guatemalan. We explained this situation earlier in this chapter and in the "Changes in Census Procedures" section of chapter 2.

Residential distribution. Many Central Americans, particularly Salvadorans, came to Los Angeles in the late 1970s

and 1980s to escape persecution and fighting in their countries. The majority of them arrived here without much education and lacking skills needed in a modern economy. Because of their low incomes, most Central Americans have had to live in relatively low-cost housing that is, ideally, not too far from work.

However, Central American proportions are generally highest in areas different from those dominated by Mexicans (Figures 5.2 and 5.4). Although the strongest Mexican areas are east of Downtown and in former agricultural-based enclaves, Central Americans are not an important component of the population of any of these areas. In the area south of Downtown Los Angeles, Mexicans are strongest in proportions east of the Harbor Freeway (Interstate 110), but Central Americans have tended to settle to the west of that freeway. In the San Fernando Valley, few Central Americans live in the large Mexican barrio of San Fernando and vicinity. Rather, they have tended to locate in Van Nuys and North Hollywood, where Mexican proportions are much lower. These major differences in distributions reflect the importance of the differing identities and social networks of Central Americans and Mexicans.

MacArthur Park, Pico-Union

Pico-Union. Just west of Downtown and the Harbor Freeway (Interstate 110), is a vaguely defined neighborhood called Pico-Union, derived from the intersection of Pico Blvd. and Union Street (Figure 5.4). The area—sometimes called Westlake for the lake in MacArthur Park—has its main commercial corridor along Alvarado Street near MacArthur Park.

Homes in this area were originally built in the first decade of the twentieth century. Like other older, centrally located residential areas in American cities, decisions by most homeowners and potential buyers over the last half century to move to the suburbs led to lowered demand for properties in this area and thus declining real estate investment. As property values fell and houses and apartment buildings deteriorated, this hous-

ing came within the reach of poorer people who, since about 1970, were mostly Latino immigrants and their families.

This area contains both Mexicans and Central Americans, but for Central Americans this has been an especially important destination. The location of the area is convenient for some people's employment. Many Central Americans work in Downtown as janitors cleaning high-rise office buildings or dressmakers in sweatshops of the Garment District or in other jobs. For others it is less convenient. Many neighborhood women who are maids and nannies in places like Beverly Hills, Brentwood, and Santa Monica must take buses for a long ride to and from work.

As the number of Central Americans in Pico-Union grew, especially during the 1980s, restaurants, markets, health clinics, and a range of retail or service businesses opened. Soccer clubs are popular; and several churches, including charismatic Catholic and Evangelical Protestant, minister particularly to Central Americans.[19] The enclave has became large enough to satisfy most needs of residents.

Central Americans who live some distance away from the Pico-Union area do not go to there to shop, visit, or obtain services.[20] It is a poor area and not attractive. Moreover, because rental units and apartment buildings are often poorly maintained and because crime, drugs, and gangs make life difficult, many residents would prefer to be living in better neighborhoods—but simply can't afford rents in those places.

Central Americans have expanded their Pico-Union enclave—both to the northwest into the less expensive, eastern parts of Hollywood and southward into South Central, particularly the area along Vermont and Western Avenues and near the campus of the University of Southern California (Figure 5.4). Central Americans are replacing Blacks who are departing that part of South Central north of the Santa Monica Freeway (Interstate 10). In the poorer parts of Hollywood, Central Americans are a component in an ethnically varied population including elderly Whites and Thai, Filipino, and Armenian immigrants. The westward expansion of Central American settlement appears to have been blocked by Koreatown.

The San Fernando Valley and other areas. The San Fernando Valley probably represents the most important residential area for the more economically successful Central Americans and the development of Central American institutions.[21] Van Nuys, Panorama City, and North Hollywood are particularly significant locations. Not surprisingly, the portions of the Valley where over 10 percent of the total population is Central American are relatively low-income areas that have higher proportions of apartment buildings.[22] A great range of available jobs in the San Fernando Valley is also, of course, a necessary factor in people's decision to locate there.

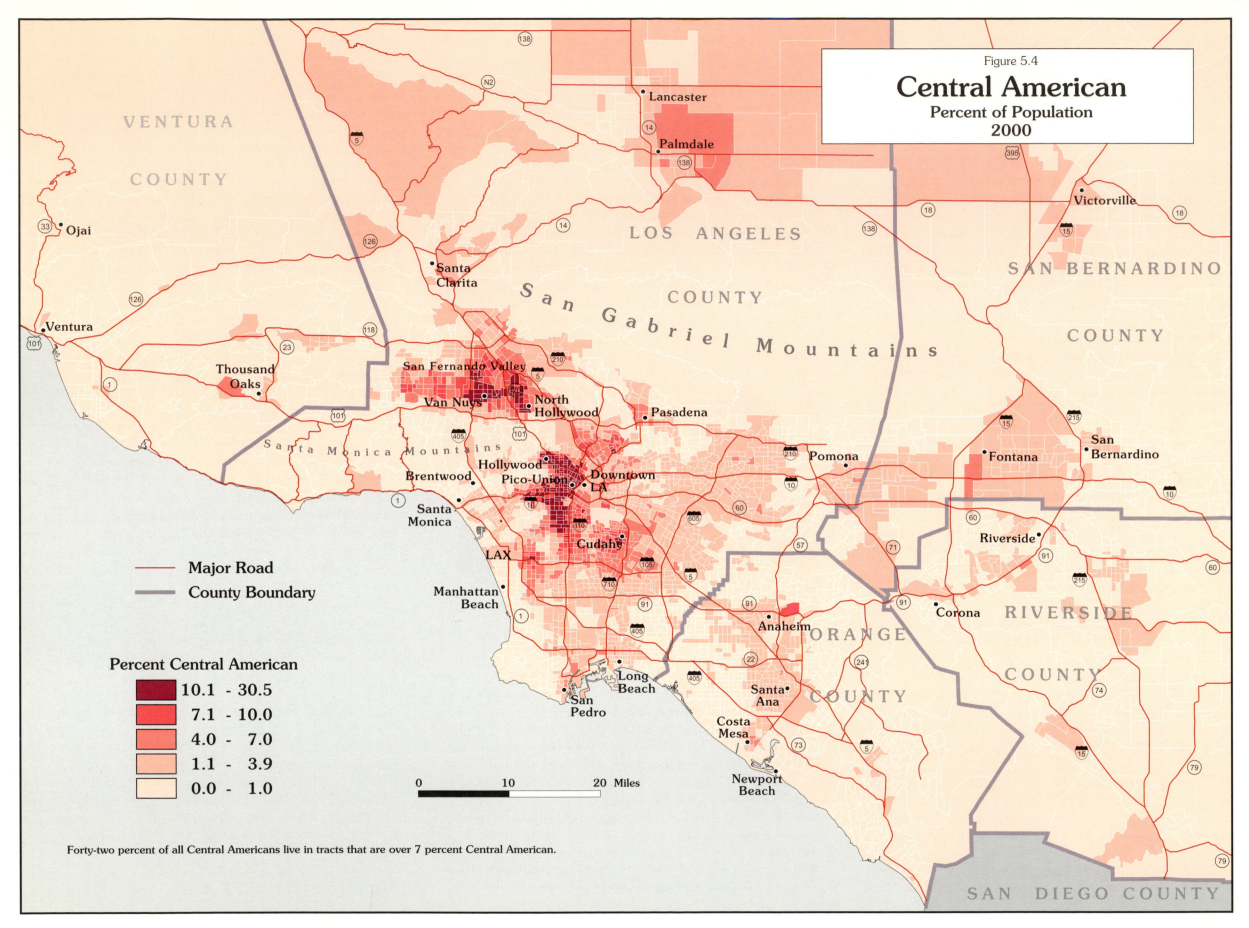

Figure 5.4

Central American
Percent of Population
2000

Percent Central American

▮	10.1 – 30.5
▮	7.1 – 10.0
▮	4.0 – 7.0
▮	1.1 – 3.9
▯	0.0 – 1.0

—— Major Road

—— County Boundary

0   10   20 Miles

Forty-two percent of all Central Americans live in tracts that are over 7 percent Central American.

The importance of the San Fernando Valley for Central Americans is reflected in the recent establishment of a Central American Studies Program at California State University, Northridge. The program focuses on understanding Central America and its growing linkages with Southern California and the rest of the world.

Individual census tracts with high percentages of Central Americans result from the fact that fellow Central Americans often provide helpful directions to specific apartment buildings, neighborhoods, and jobs to people they know. Because their networks are usually different from those of Mexicans, the net geographical effect is to concentrate nationality groups in certain neighborhoods, such as in the city of Cudahy, in Lennox just east of LAX, and in Anaheim and Fontana (Figure 5.4).

Some localized ethnic concentrations would sometimes be more evident if maps showed varying ethnic percentages by blocks rather than census tracts. This can be the case where neighborhood character and housing prices vary substantially within a census tract. In the generally affluent city of Thousand Oaks in Ventura County is a tract with a percentage of Central Americans between 4 and 7 percent (Figure 5.4). They are actually highly concentrated in a few blocks, one of which is 76-percent Latino. The neighborhood contains small but attractive and well landscaped apartment buildings, but the price of housing is low for that city. It is probable that word of this housing opportunity spread among many Central Americans and others who may work nearby.

Latino Enclaves

When Central Americans, Cubans, and South Americans are included with Mexicans, some strongly Latino neighborhoods become particularly evident (Figure 5.3). As Whites and, in some cases Blacks, have been leaving many of these poorer areas for two or more decades, some sections of Southern

Table 5.2. Enclave Settlement of Latinos, 1990 and 2000: Los Angeles CMSA

Percent Latino in Tracts	Percent Latinos in Each Category		Change 1990-2000
	1990	2000	
80 – 100%	24.0	26.6	+2.6
60 – 79%	21.1	24.9	+3.8
40 – 59%	18.9	23.0	+4.1
20 – 39%	22.2	17.1	-5.1
0 – 19%	13.8	8.4	-5.4

Sources: 1990 U.S. Census STF1; Census 2000 Hispanic tables.

California are over 80 percent Latino. There are also neighborhoods in which over 95 percent of the people are Latino.

Latinos during the 1990s became more likely to be living in census tracts that were 40 percent Latino or higher (Table 5.2). This is a clear demonstration of the increase in enclave settlement among Latinos. Because the percentage of Latinos in Southern California grew during the 1990s, a small increase in the percentage of Latinos in all categories should be expected. The fact of a higher proportion living in enclaves is clearly demonstrated by the decline in the percentage of Latinos living in tracts less than 40 percent Latino.

These findings are consistent with the slightly increased White-Latino residential separation observed in 2000 compared to 1990 when measured by the index of dissimilarity (Table 7.2). The growing Latino enclaves in Southern California are also clearly related to the 38-percent growth in numbers of foreign-born from Latin America and the 35-percent growth in numbers of Spanish speakers who could not speak English very well.[23]

Table 5.3. Enclave Settlement of Latino Groups, 1990 and 2000: Los Angeles CMSA

Group	Threshold for Enclaves		Percent in Enclaves		Change 1990-2000
	1990	2000	1990	2000	
Mexican	25.7	30.3	72.2	73.8	+1.6
Central Amer.	10.5	8.0	49.8	37.5	-12.3

Sources: 1990 U.S. Census STF1; Census 2000 Hispanic tables.

Notes: According to Census 2000 figures, Central Americans constituted 3.5% of the total five-county population in 1990 and 2.7% in 2000. These values were multiplied by 3 to define the threshold for an ethnic enclave, as explained in chapter 1. The reduction in percentage from 1990 to 2000 results primarily from changes in census questionnaire wording, as explained in chapter 2. However, that data problem does not affect our calculations of enclave percentages. Due to the large size of the Mexican population, we calculated thresholds for enclave settlement as simply the percentage Mexican in the total population. This was 25.7% of the total five-county population in 1990 and 30.3% in 2000.

Because Mexicans comprise about 80 percent of Latinos in Southern California, Table 5.2 reflects primarily trends among Mexicans. When Mexican enclave settlement is measured directly (Table 5.3), the proportion of Mexicans living in enclaves grew from about 72 to about 74 percent. This small increase in enclave settlement implies that the processes of residential concentration and deconcentration were almost balanced during the 1990s. Nevertheless, processes leading toward increased concentration were more powerful than opposing tendencies toward dispersal. This was presumably because the enclave settlement of recent Mexican immigrants more than balanced the dispersal associated with the assimilation of earlier immigrants and U.S.-born Mexicans.

On the other hand Central Americans deconcentrated residentially during the 1990s. This dispersal from enclaves has been very strong, as is evident by the fact that the percentage of Central Americans living in enclaves declined substantially even though the threshold for enclave settlement also declined. This residential dispersal could have been mostly into Mexican areas, considering the somewhat shared culture including the use of "Spanish". However, the distinct distributions of Mexicans and Central Americans (Figures 5.2 and 5.4) suggest this was less common than dispersal into mostly White or more ethnically diverse neighborhoods. To the extent that the latter is true, the shift implies cultural and/or economic assimilation into the mainstream society.

American Indians

Because there are so few Eskimos, Aleuts, and Alaskan Indians in Southern California, we do not treat those Alaska Natives in our interpretation. Southern California contains a much larger urban Indian population than any other metropolitan area, and since 1970 Los Angeles County has had more Indians than any other county in the United States. The next largest Indian center is New York, but the five-county Los Angeles metropolitan area (CMSA) contains 70 percent more Indians than the comparable New York CMSA.

Difficulties in defining and counting Indians. The numbers that we and the Census Bureau provide may give an erroneous impression of precision that isn't justified by the mixed backgrounds and identities of most urban Indians. Usually Indians establish their identities and are accepted as Indians by other Indians more on the basis of active participation in Indian community affairs than through some blood quantum or genealogy-derived percentage measure.[24]

In Census 2000 the determination of any single total for American Indians is particularly complicated by the large proportion that reported themselves as both American Indian and another race. In the five counties of Southern California a total of 142,083 people considered themselves only American Indian, but another 116,906 marked both Indian and another one or more races.

In the "New mixed-race data" section of chapter 2 we explain why fractionally assigning multiracial people into their appropriate single-race groups is a fair, straightforward, and reasonable way to arrive at a total that can be compared to the 1990 count.[25] In the case of mixed-race Indians, we assigned them in equal fractions into the single-race groups that they marked on the census questionnaire. This means that persons who identified themselves as both Indian and White would be apportioned one-half to each group and those who were mixed

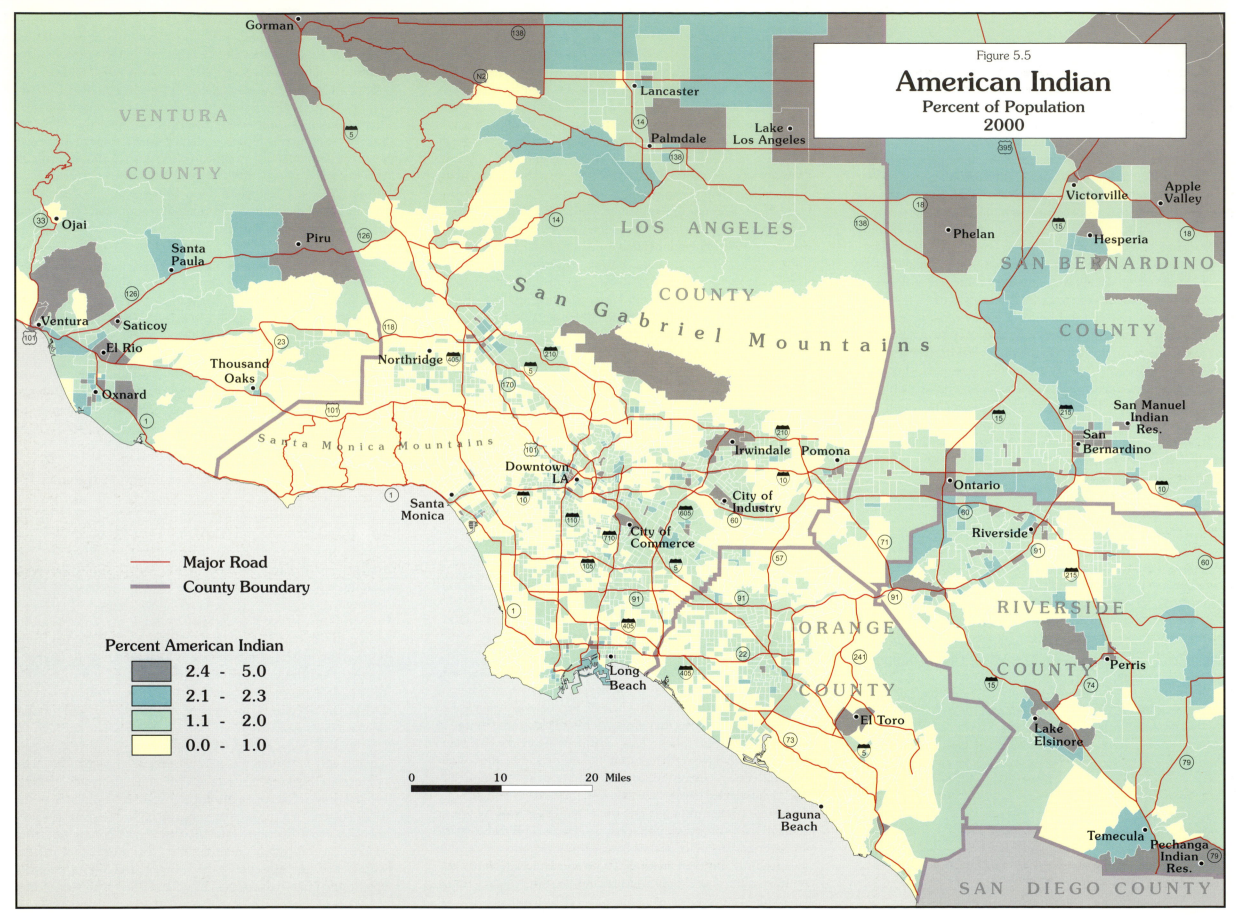

Figure 5.5

American Indian
Percent of Population
2000

Percent American Indian

- 2.4 – 5.0
- 2.1 – 2.3
- 1.1 – 2.0
- 0.0 – 1.0

Major Road

County Boundary

Indian-White-Black would be apportioned one-third to each of those groups.

Growth of Indian numbers in the 1990s. Using this procedure, we calculated a total of about 197,000 Indians in Southern California as of 2000 (Table 3.2). This appears at first to represent more than a doubling of the 88,000 Indians counted in 1990, but this is not the case. Some of the increased numbers resulted from the new opportunity for many Whites and Blacks to report also an Indian identity, which we accounted for in our fractional assignment. Another part of the unusual increase may be due to an undercount of Indians in 1990.[26]

If the 1990 count is accepted, however, the fact that 142,000 Southern Californians reported themselves in 2000 as only Indian (i.e., not mixed-race) suggests that Indian numbers grew by at least 60 percent during the 1990s. Even allowing for a substantial 1990 undercount, the number of Indians living in Southern California has increased greatly in recent years. One small factor in this growth—apart from in-migration and natural increase—could be a continuation of the trend observed since 1970 for many Americans to switch their main identity on the census questionnaire from White, Black, or some other race to American Indian.[27]

Indigenous Southern California Indians. Indians native to Southern California were devastated by the conquering Spanish, Mexican, and United States governments and by in-migrating White residents. We do not attempt to treat this tortured history.[28] By the 1970s, Southern California had many small numbers of indigenous Indians and tiny, scattered reservations (rancherias).

Within the five counties examined here, Riverside and San Bernardino Counties have the most important settlements and reservations. The two in the area mapped (Figure 5.5) are the one-square-mile San Manuel Reservation east of San Bernardino and the approximately six-square-mile Pechanga Reservation southeast of Temecula. Both of the census tracts that contain these are less than 5-percent Indian in population. To the east, however, in the tract that includes the Soboba Reservation about 17 percent of the people reported themselves as Indian in 2000.

The low Indian percentages in rural areas is partly due to the small Indian populations on or near reservations.[29] For example, about 85 Serrano Indians live on the San Manuel Reservation, but Serranos also live on or near the Morongo and Soboba Reservations. Luiseño Indians associated with reservations in Riverside and San Diego Counties totaled about 1,800 in 1990, but they were separated geographically into smaller groups including the Pala, Pechanga, Pauma, Rincon, and Soboba tribes. Similarly, in 1990 a total of almost 1,300

Cahuilla Indians lived on several separate reservations: Agua Caliente, Cabazon, Cahuilla, Morongo, Ramona, Santa Rosa, Torres-Martinez, and others. Some Chumash are in Ventura and Los Angeles Counties although their only reservation is in northern Santa Barbara County. Indians from these indigenous tribes are likely to be living within the urban area of greater Los Angeles, but they are rarely noticed by non-Indians.[30]

Nowadays, some of the indigenous Indians are best known to other Southern Californians for the gaming casinos that they have developed, mostly during the 1990s. Nevada-style gaming is permitted on these reservations, and the location of some makes them an attractive alternative for people who would otherwise fly or drive to Las Vegas. The largest within the area mapped (Figure 5.5) is the Pechanga Casino, which has slot machines, gaming tables, restaurants, an entertainment center featuring musicians and other performers, and a large new hotel. Farther east in Riverside County is the hard-to-miss Casino Morongo on Interstate 10 at Cabezon. Other casinos include the Soboba, the Cahuilla Creek, and the Chumash. Altogether, the wealth generated by gaming profits has opened new opportunities for Southern California Indians and has give them more influence politically.[31]

Indians from elsewhere in the United States. In the 1950s the federal government instituted a Job Relocation Program that persuaded many Indians to leave their reservations and move to cities where jobs were more plentiful.[32] Although the program failed, partly because adequate job training was not provided, it prompted thousands of Indians to move into large urban areas like Los Angeles.

The net effect has been that indigenous Southern California groups are now greatly outnumbered by Indians such as Apache, Cherokee, Choctaw, Navajo, Sioux and others.[33] Contemporary Indian life in urban Southern California includes traditional elements from many Indian cultures and is mostly pan-Indian or intertribal. It is best known for the frequent Saturday powwows—public social gatherings, with dancers and participants from many different tribes and booths from which Indian handicrafts and food are sold.[34]

Distribution in Southern California. Thus, the distribution (Figure 5.5) reflects primarily the locations of a wide range of Indian groups from across the United States rather than the settlements of indigenous tribes. What is striking about this distribution is the lack of Indian settlement clusters or enclaves. No census tract on the map has a population that is more than five-percent American Indian, and Indian percentages vary only slightly across the map.

Indians comprise a slightly higher percentage of local residents in rural, low-density areas where housing costs are not

high—in Piru, Saticoy, and El Rio in Ventura County; and a variety of places in northern Los Angeles County and in Riverside and San Bernardino Counties (Figure 5.5). City neighborhoods with lower-priced housing (Irwindale, City of Industry, Ontario) also sometimes show Indian proportions that are greater than 2.4 percent. It appears that Indians are mixed residentially with Latinos in many such neighborhoods. In contrast, fewer Indians live in very affluent areas such as the Santa Monica Mountains, the Palos Verdes Peninsula, and southern Orange County.

Indian enclaves have always been weak in urban Los Angeles. As of 1970 there was a slight Indian concentration in the Bell Gardens-Huntington Park area, partly a function of earlier Cherokee settlement among Whites from Oklahoma in this area. In the 1980s Indians tended to disperse slightly from older, more central city locations such as these and from Lynwood and Anaheim. Indians moved into both older suburban cities like Bellflower, San Gabriel and Alhambra and more distant places like the eastern San Gabriel Valley, Lancaster, Palmdale, and Dana Point.[35] Such a centrifugal shift seemed to reflect a slight improvement in economic circumstances.

Aztec dancer at a powwow

Hispanic Indians. In addition to their identity as American Indians and, for many, some other race as well, 60 percent of Indians in Southern California in 2000 reported themselves as Hispanic or Latino.[36] Because in 1990 only 32 percent of Southern California Indians were of Hispanic origin, some significant change occurred during the 1990s. It seems likely that this increasing Hispanic proportion had two major causes. First, there has been an increasing immigration of Indians from Mexico and Central America.[37] This immigration of Central American (mostly Guatemalan) and Mexican Indians has been taking place since the mid-1970s but may well have grown during the 1990s. Second, the larger number of Hispanic Indians results partly from the increasing identification of Californians of Mexican heritage—including many university students—with their indigenous Indian roots.[38]

Mexican Indians in Ventura County. Many Indians from the poor, rural states of Oaxaca, Guerrero, and Chiapas in Southern Mexico have made their way into Ventura County—often illegally. They harvest crops from the rich, irrigated fields of the Oxnard Plain or work as day laborers or landscapers.[39] Some Indians from Mexico, like other poor Mexicans, have been recruited by agents of California growers.[40] The growers know that the severe poverty of Indians often makes them desperate and thus willing to work for very low wages and in poor conditions. It is likely that reports of farm labor work in Southern California have spread through the Indians' social networks, making recruiting less necessary. These Indians are the latest in a long series of groups that have provided the labor on California farms for over a century.

For many Mixtec Indians from the state of Oaxaca, Southern California is an extension northward of earlier migration streams into intensive farming areas within Mexico like that of San Quintin in Baja California. Many Mixtec who pick strawberries in Ventura County follow the crops north, picking blackberries in Oregon and returning south in November to the San Joaquin Valley to pick table grapes.[41] The Indians—many of whom speak neither English nor Spanish—are isolated socially and subject to much discrimination from both Spanish and English speakers.

Mexican and Guatemalan Indians in Los Angeles. Thousands of Mexican and Guatemalan Indians live in Los Angeles County. Young Indian men from Oaxaca learned to love basketball back home, and there are enough Oaxacan Indian players here to support over forty basketball tournaments here each year.[42]

Many Guatemalan Indians in Los Angeles work in the garment industry, often sewing dresses on the upper floors of old buildings near Downtown Los Angeles.[43] Other Mexican Indians work as dishwashers, kitchen assistants, and bus boys, often in Westside restaurants.[44] Some Indians from Oaxaca have developed their own businesses in Los Angeles.

Mexican and Central American Indians live in many parts of the L.A. area. Until the last few years newly arrived Maya Indians from Guatemala would typically locate close to each other, finding apartments in a few blocks along Bixel Street in the poor, mostly Latino Pico-Union area just west of the Harbor Freeway (Interstate 110).[45] However, in recent years many Indians have left those crowded tenements and dangerous streets. Seeking more rooms, safer neighborhoods, and better schools for their children, many have moved to places like South Central L.A. and the San Fernando Valley. Such residential shifts on the part of the Maya are consistent with our finding of reduced enclave settlement among Central Americans.

Notes

1. The White-Mexican gap in median income has clearly grown wider since 1960 (Allen and Turner 1997, 173, 195-198; Allen 2002). However, some Latinos have found paths toward socioeconomic progress. Clark (2001) found evidence in California of both increasing income inequality among Latinos and growing numbers of Latinos in the middle-class. Others are having great difficulty. As assessed by López and Stanton-Salazar (2001, 58), "The socioeconomic disadvantages and dismal school performance of the Mexican-origin second generation are particularly striking in California, where other contemporary immigrant groups are notable for just the opposite."

2. The Current Population Survey of March 2000, in comparison to 1990 census figures, showed that the Mexican foreign-born population of the United States increased by 82 percent during the 1990s. In contrast, the Mexican foreign-born population in the five counties of Southern California increased by only 23 percent (U.S. Census Bureau 2001d; U.S. Census Bureau 1993c). Such very different growth rates could have resulted from either increased migration of foreign-born Mexicans out of Southern California to other parts of the United States or a reduced attractiveness of Southern California as a destination for newly arriving Mexican immigrants or some combination of these factors.

3. California Department of Finance (2001). See also Johnson, Hill, and Heim (2001), 7.

4. These problems and the superior Pew estimates (Suro 2002) are explained in the "Changes in Census Procedures" section of chapter 2. The Pew Hispanic Center's report "Counting the "Other Hispanics" also contains estimates for most Hispanic nationalities (e.g., Guatemalans and Chileans) for the U.S. and for the Los Angeles CMSA.

5. Rodriguez (1996); Clark (2001).

6. Virginia Parks, resident of Venice and Ph.D. student in Geography at UCLA, explained the recent gentrification in detail, April 2002.

7. William Davis of the Housing Authority of the City of Los Angeles explained this development, April 2002. See also Johnson (2002).

8. The five tracts in Boyle Heights are 2031, 2032, 2042, 2044, and 2051; the Pico-Union tracts are 2094.03 and 2098.02.

9. See footnote 2.

10. Such pressures on apartment residents who are ethnically different from the building's owners have been widely reported at Fair Housing Council offices. See also Fox (2001).

11. We include here only maps of Mexicans and Central Americans because these are by far the largest Latino groups in Southern California. However, 1990 maps showing Cuban, Puerto Rican, and South American distributions can be found in Allen and Turner (1997).

12. Sánchez (1993), 198-201.

13. Myers (2002).

14. Zierer (1934).

15. Bloom (1959).

16. Dagodag (1967).

17. U.S. Census Bureau (1993c), Table 185.

18. For details on the Orange County *colonias* see Gonzales (1994).

19. Hamilton and Chinchilla (2001), 168-169.

20. Roberto Lovato, former director of the Central American Refugee Center in Pico-Union, made this observation.

21. Roberto Lovato of CSU Northridge stressed the importance of the San Fernando Valley for Central Americans.

22. Allen and Turner (1997), 24, 107.

23. U.S. Census Bureau (1993d), Tables 27, 28; U.S. Census Bureau (2002c), Table DP-2.

24. Gonzalez (2001), 179.

25. For further information on fractional assignment of mixed-race populations beyond that explained in chapter 2, see our methodologically detailed article (Allen and Turner 2001).

26. Weibel-Orlando (1999), 278-279, 296.

27. Passel (1996), 86.

28. The tragic history of Southern California Indians is poignantly summarized in Bonvillain (2001).

29. White (2001).

30. Fascinating life histories of three Cupeño Indian women in a family living in Huntington Park are presented by an anthropologist in Bahr (1993).

31. Bonvillain (2001), 415.

32. Bonvillain (2001).

33. Allen and Turner (1997), 91.

34. The most thorough analysis of powwows can be found in Weibel-Orlando (1999), 132-152. That book also covers many additional features of Indian culture and politics in Los Angeles.

35. Weibel-Orlando (1999), 287-292.

36. This figure is based on those who marked only the race category "American Indian". The 60 percent figure would be even higher if Hispanic Indians who reported two or more races were included. U.S. Census Bureau, American FactFinder, Detailed Tables, P8. http://factfinder.census.gov/

37. We suspect also that some partial acculturation of the children of Indians who immigrated in the 1980s resulted in a higher rate of response to Census 2000 than to that of 1990. In addition, a Census Bureau analysis indicates that a change in the wording of the questionnaire in 2000 was a likely factor in eliciting more Hispanic Indian responses than in 1990. In 1990 the questionnaire showed "Indian (Amer.)" as the racial category, but in 2000 the clearer phrase "American Indian" was used. See Martin (2002). Although United States residents sometimes assume the word "American" applies just to the United States, people in Latin America also consider themselves American. Considering this, it should not be surprising to find Indians from Latin America identifying as "American Indian".

38. Karren Baird-Olson of CSU Northridge pointed out this important identity development among our students.

39. Alvarez (1995).

40. Krissman (2000).

41. Hubner (2001).

42. Quinones (2001), 117-135.

43. Hamilton and Chinchilla (2001), 80.

44. Quinones (2001), 119-120.

45. Loucky (2000, 2001).

6. Asians and Pacific Islanders

Wat Thai Buddhist temple, North Hollywood

The five-county Southern California area has the largest Asian population of any metropolitan area in the United States. It has been growing rapidly since about 1970, primarily through immigration. In 1980 Asians comprised less than 3 percent of Southern Californians, but by 2000 they represented over 11 percent (derived from Table 3.2). Although much less numerous than Latinos or Whites, they have outnumbered Blacks in Southern California since the late 1980s.

Asians and Pacific Islanders is an aggregation that includes people of very different languages and cultural heritages. They are more diverse culturally than Latinos, who are unified to some degree by a common Spanish language background.

In both Southern California and the United States as a whole, Chinese and Filipinos are the two largest Asian groups (Table 6.1). Los Angeles County is easily the leading center for Filipinos and Koreans in the country, as is Orange County for Vietnamese. However, for Chinese and Japanese Los Angeles County is only the second largest center because Chinese in the five boroughs of New York City slightly outnumber those in Los Angeles County, and Honolulu County (Oahu) is the largest Japanese concentration in the country.

Asian Indians are the third largest Asian group in the United States, but in Southern California their numbers are less than in either New York or Chicago. This is because older immigrant pathways and recent high-tech employment opportunities have directed them more to other areas. Because their numbers in Southern California are so much less than the five leading groups, we do not map them specifically.

Asian Indians and smaller groups such as Thais, Cambodians, and Samoans were covered in *The Ethnic Quilt* and are not treated here. The chapter title includes Pacific Islanders, as does our map of population change during the 1990s, because we wished to be inclusive in our coverage. Nevertheless, Pacific Islanders comprise less than 3 percent of all Asians and Pacific Islanders in Southern California. For this reason we simplify the terminology by using "Asian" for the entire Asian and Pacific Islander aggregation.

Racially Mixed Asians

The Census 2000 counts of specific Asian groups include the numbers reporting some Asian race and another race, but they do not identify the specific races with which Asian groups are mixed. For this reason the mixed-race populations could not

be fractionally assigned in order to make possible the calculation of rates of population change for the 1990s. (See chapter 2 regarding these mixed-race data and methods of handling them.) There are alternative 2000 counts of Asian groups depending on whether mixed-race Asians are included and how they are tabulated (Table 6.1, columns 2-4).

Regardless of the data used, however, it appears that the Chinese, Filipino, Korean, and Vietnamese populations grew rapidly in Southern California during the 1990s. Asian Indians increased also, especially in Orange County. Japanese, on the other hand, showed much less growth.

Some people reporting mixed-Asian backgrounds (Table 6.1, column 3) are ethnic Chinese from various Southeast Asian countries. For example, many individuals marked both "Vietnamese" and "Chinese" on the census questionnaire to show both their ethnic identity and the country in which they formerly lived. Thus, dual Asian identities do not necessarily reflect past ethnic intermarriage.

Despite the problems of measuring trends with the Census 2000 data, the new mixed-race data can be analyzed in terms of ethnic and county differences (Table 6.1). Column (5), representing the percentage of all members of the Asian group that reported also at least one non-Asian race, provides a useful measure of varying mixed-race proportions. Although ethnic groups may differ in the emphasis placed upon marriage within their ethnic group, a more important factor explaining group variations in racial mixing is probably the average length of time the group has lived in the United States. This is because in the United States there is much exposure to different racial groups and relatively more opportunity for marriage outside one's own ethnic group than in the Asian countries of origin.

In all five counties, the Japanese are more likely to report a mixed-race heritage than the other Asian groups. This is consistent with the longer Japanese experience in this country, the group's lower percentage of foreign-born (immigrants) compared to U.S.-born, and its higher rate of intermarriage compared

Table 6.1. Major Asian Populations, 1990 and 2000: Counties in Los Angeles CMSA

	1990	2000 Race alone	2000 Mixed with an Asian race	2000 Mixed with a non-Asian race	2000 Percent mixed with a non-Asian race
	(1)	(2)	(3)	(4)	(5)
Los Angeles County					
Asian Indian	43,829	60,268	2,703	8,294	11.6
Cambodian	27,819	28,226	2,407	3,399	10.0
Chinese	245,033	329,352	29,143	19,208	5.1
Filipino	219,653	260,158	6,203	30,347	10.2
Japanese	129,739	111,349	5,905	20,826	15.1
Korean	145,431	186,350	2,625	6,175	3.2
Thai	19,016	20,040	1,376	2,735	11.3
Vietnamese	62,594	78,102	8,186	2,792	3.1
Orange County					
Asian Indian	15,212	27,197	810	2,457	8.1
Chinese	41,403	59,717	6,916	5,804	8.0
Filipino	30,356	48,946	1,619	9,435	15.7
Japanese	29,704	31,283	1,909	8,575	20.5
Korean	35,919	55,573	740	2,251	3.8
Vietnamese	71,822	135,548	2,997	2,619	1.9
Riverside County					
Chinese	4,704	6,590	926	1,723	18.6
Filipino	12,748	20,850	511	5,498	20.5
Japanese	3,920	4,062	229	3,002	41.2
Korean	3,877	5,336	92	846	13.5
Vietnamese	4,618	6,612	351	423	5.7
San Bernardino County					
Chinese	8,462	12,580	1,553	2,242	13.7
Filipino	16,171	25,919	580	5,735	17.8
Japanese	5,046	4,425	314	3,226	40.5
Korean	6,289	7,407	165	1,098	12.7
Vietnamese	6,697	10,003	372	556	5.1
Ventura County					
Chinese	4,986	6,343	511	1,266	15.6
Filipino	12,690	15,548	296	3,136	16.5
Japanese	4,964	4,840	249	2,304	31.2
Korean	2,921	3,309	87	444	11.6
Vietnamese	2,486	3,308	111	211	5.8

Sources: 1990 Census: 100-percent-count data (U.S. Census Bureau 1993a). Census 2000: 100-percent count data from SF1. http://factfinder.census.gov/

Notes: Chinese includes Taiwanese. Data are reported for the five largest Asian groups in each county plus any other Asian group numbering 20,000 or more in any county in 2000. The three columns of 2000 data show the number reporting only that specific Asian race, the number reporting that specific Asian race mixed with another Asian race, and a number reporting that specific Asian race mixed with a non-Asian race.

to other Asian groups except Thais.[1] Vietnamese and Koreans, on the other hand, represent more recent immigration flows. Their mixed-race proportions are lower than other Asian groups as a result of fewer years in the United States and, therefore, less opportunity to marry outside the group.

Place differences in the rates of racial mixing reflect the absolute size of the group's population in different places. Los Angeles and Orange Counties tend to have lower percentages of mixed-race Asians. This is partly because the large numbers in each ethnic group and the greater development of residential concentrations or enclaves in those two counties create many opportunities for marriage within the group. In general, rates of racial mixing for different counties may be an important indicator of society's relative openness and fluidity as opposed ethnic separation or compartmentalization in those places.

Riverside and San Bernardino Counties have higher proportions of racially mixed Asians than the other counties. The attractiveness of those counties for such racially mixed people may be partly related to the recent rapid growth in those counties and their lack of established Asian neighborhoods dating from the era of racial segregation. New Asian arrivals in those counties are probably also younger and less concerned with traditional separations between ethnic groups. The highest percentage of racially mixed Asian is reached among Japanese in Riverside and San Bernardino Counties, where over 40 percent of Japanese identified also with another race (usually White).

Thus, the evidence from Census 2000 of place differences in racially mixed proportions is quite clear. Newer suburban areas, with fewer members of each group and perhaps less traditional attitudes concerning ethnic separation, have tended to attract racially mixed Asians.

Asian Population Change

Growth and dispersal. Asians in Southern California increased by one-third (over 400,000) in the 1990s. Much of this growth was dispersed in suburban areas, such as new developments in Ventura County and in southern Orange County (Figure 6.1). Such dispersed settlement tends to attract those who are more comfortable with the English language and mainstream American culture.[2]

The maps accentuate the areas where immigrants have settled because they are the leading source of Asian growth. However, large numbers of Asians and, in particular, community leaders were born in the United States. This population typically resides outside the ethnic enclaves, usually in some suburb of either Los Angeles City or that county. Such highly assimilated, successful Asians play very important roles, but their presence is not revealed in the maps.

Enclave expansion. At the same time, growing clusters of Asian settlement are very evident. Ethnic residential concentrations or enclaves are attractive to many people because their neighbors are more likely to be friends and relatives and because ethnic markets, businesses, professional services, and cultural institutions are more accessible. Recent immigrants often feel more at home living in enclaves.

Two particularly large concentrations are the mostly Chinese population in and around Monterey Park in the Western San Gabriel Valley and the Vietnamese enclave called Little Saigon, centered in Westminster and Garden Grove in Orange County (Figure 6.1). The third largest area of Asian growth during the 1990s was in the eastern San Gabriel Valley, especially in areas with newer and more expensive homes.

A similar pattern of Asian growth in more affluent neighborhoods is found over much of Southern California, particularly where local schools are known to be excellent. This educational factor has been very important for many Asians in selecting a place to live. In previous decades a mostly Japanese enclave developed in Torrance, including both Japanese Americans and Japanese nationals as residents. Some of these residents probably moved there from nearby Gardena, a much older Japanese enclave. Torrance's Asian-oriented stores, schools, and other institutions are easily accessible to Asian residents in the nearby Palos Verdes Peninsula. To the east, Cerritos, a newer affluent suburb dating mostly from the 1970s, has also been attractive to Asians from several ethnic groups.

In Orange County, Irvine has become a new Asian enclave. The city is seen as safe and its University High School is well known and highly respected.[3] The nearby University of California at Irvine—where over half the undergraduates are Asian—is also an important draw. The western part of Irvine is an "edge city" with modern office buildings and manufacturing, but to the east are upscale residential areas with homes constructed since the mid-1970s. With its distinctive high-tech employment characteristics, Irvine has clearly been attractive to computer engineers and other skilled professionals, many of whom are Asian.[4]

Closer to L.A.'s Downtown, three older and somewhat poorer Asian enclaves—Chinatown, Little Tokyo, and Koreatown—also grew somewhat during the 1990s. This is a

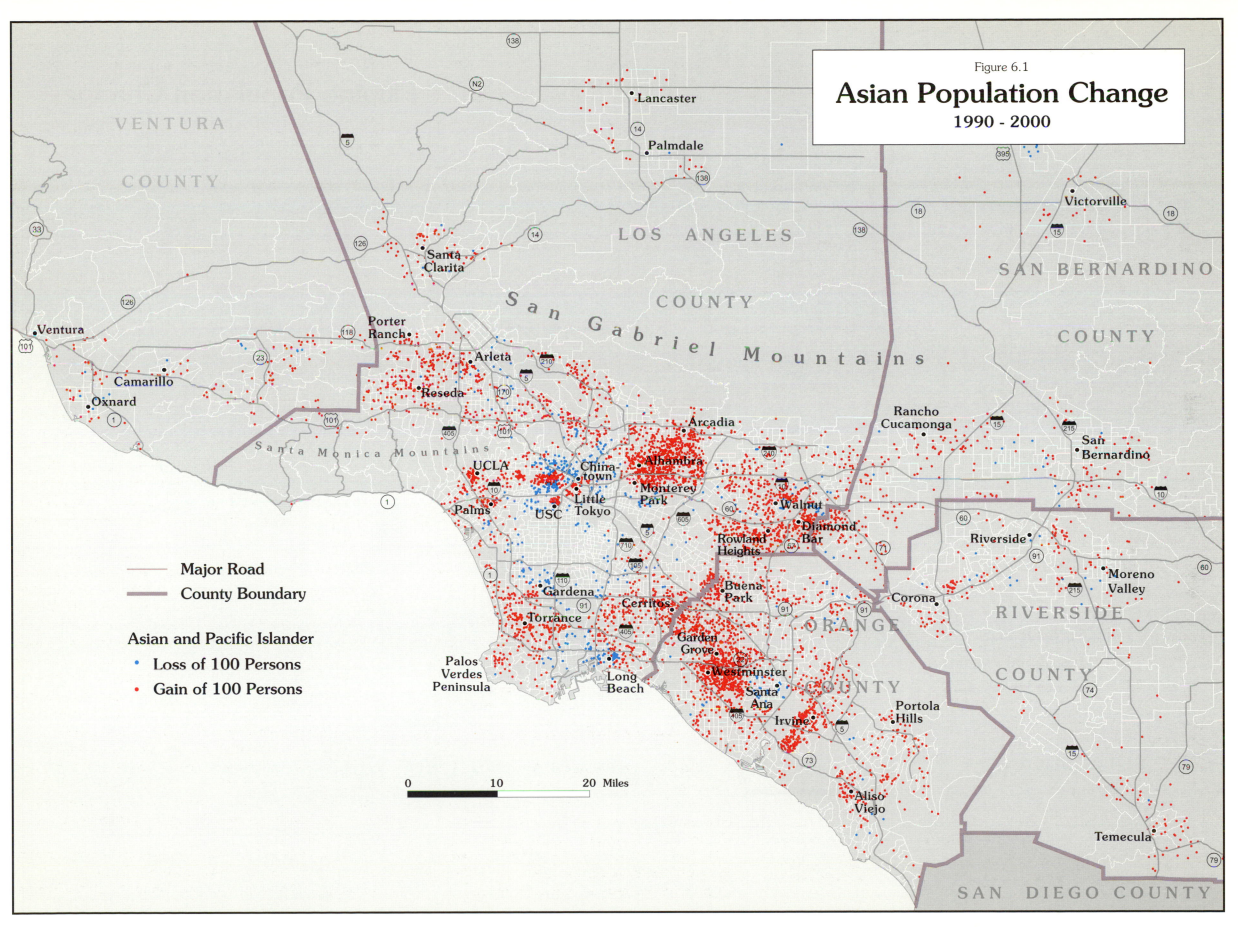

Figure 6.1
Asian Population Change
1990 - 2000

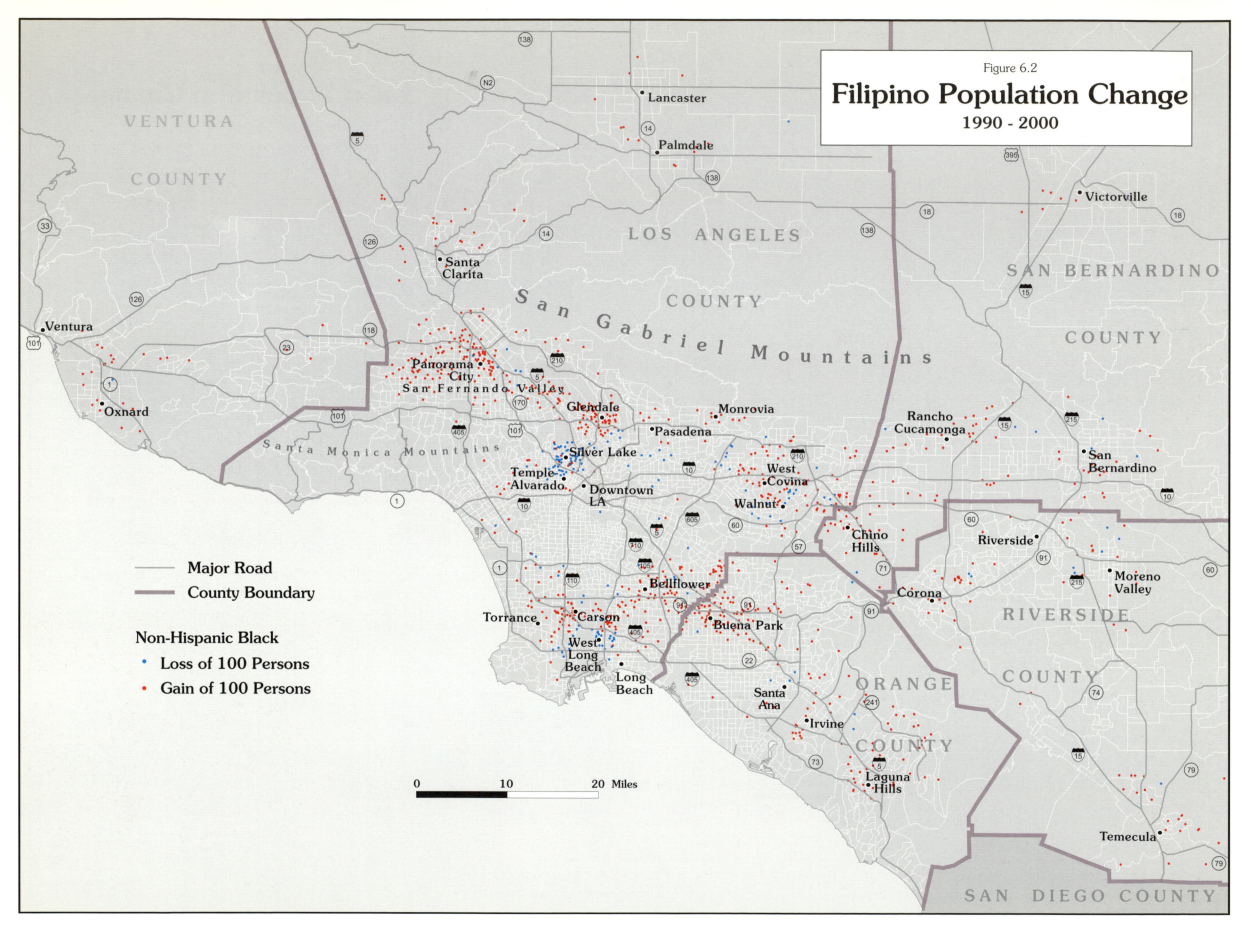

Figure 6.2
Filipino Population Change
1990 - 2000

Major Road

County Boundary

Non-Hispanic Black
• Loss of 100 Persons
• Gain of 100 Persons

0   10   20 Miles

reminder that many recent immigrants and their children cannot afford to live in more expensive areas but still want the cultural advantages and social support associated with living in an ethnic enclave.

Altogether, the Asian population increased most in newer, more affluent suburbs. Enough Asians settled in Torrance, Irvine, Cerritos, and the East San Gabriel Valley so that each of those grew in numbers and is essentially a multiethnic Asian enclave. (See "Asian Settlement in Enclaves and Changes" near the end of this chapter.)

Declining Asian settlements. In contrast, Asians tended to leave less expensive, older residential areas that were not distinctively Asian concentrations. Some of these neighborhoods had crime and gang problems. One such area lies on the east, north and west sides of L.A.'s Downtown and includes Pico-Union, Echo Park, Atwater Village, Cypress Park, Highland Park, and Boyle Heights. Similarly, Asians have been moving out of the older sections of Gardena, Hawthorne, Wilmington, Long Beach, Pomona, Santa Ana, and the northeast San Fernando Valley. In most cases, the former homes and apartments of departing Asians were occupied by Latinos, whose growing numbers created a strong demand for housing in lower-rent neighborhoods.

Filipinos

In general, the 1990s saw a net shift of Filipinos from older, poorer enclaves into economically better residential areas (Figure 6.2). Newly arrived Filipino immigrants seeking low-rent areas were apparently fewer in number than those leaving for better neighborhoods, reflecting a higher economic status for more recent immigrants. In many cases this residential change represented dispersal into newer suburbs, but in others the movement was into multiethnic Asian enclaves.

Patterns of population decline. The oldest Filipino enclave is the Temple-Alvarado area, located west of Downtown Los Angeles and just north of the expanding Latino neighborhood of Pico-Union. Filipinos settled first in this area over half a century ago when they were much poorer and were rarely permitted to rent elsewhere. The area has been declining over recent decades so that Filipinos still residing there tend to be older, less educated, and poorer than most Filipinos in Southern California.

Filipino population decreases are also evident in neighborhoods that developed originally in connection with the United States Navy. For most of the twentieth century, ambitious Filipino high school graduates competed for positions in the U.S. Navy. They typically began as stewards or in some other

menial position, but often re-enlisted for better training and pay.[5] Many later married and brought wives from the Philippines, followed by various family members, to their assigned navy bases. Thus, all the larger naval installations around the United States have local Filipino communities. The two major concentrations connected with the navy are Oxnard and Long Beach (Figure 6.3). A third and smaller navy-related Filipino tract is the Naval Weapons Station in Seal Beach just east of Long Beach, although in 2000 only about 60 Filipinos lived there in navy housing.

In the Oxnard area is another navy-related Filipino enclave which declined during the 1990s. Although some Filipinos were employed in Oxnard during the 1930s as farm workers, the thriving Filipino community in the Oxnard area probably originated in conjunction with the development of the U.S. Naval Construction Battalion Center (Seabee base) at Port Hueneme in 1942.[6] Because Filipinos played significant roles at all naval installations, further in-migration followed the construction of a naval air station and missile test center at Pt. Mugu in the early 1950s. Until the 1980s most Filipinos lived in the "Little Manila" enclave in south Oxnard, defined in 2000 by the two tracts that are over 20 percent Filipino (Figure 6.3). However, with economic success and assimilation has come the ability for Filipinos, often the children or grandchildren of Navy men, to move into newer suburban areas nearby.[7]

The drop in the Filipino population near the harbors of Long Beach and Los Angeles was the result of improved economic status and the closure of the Long Beach Naval Shipyard and the nearby naval facilities in the 1990s (Figure 6.2). The reduced Filipino numbers are mostly evident in one tract in West Long Beach where the navy had special housing for its personnel and their families.

Enclaves. Filipinos increased their numbers in moderate- and higher-priced neighborhoods, many of which are in or near established concentrations. The result is that Filipino enclaves are clearly evident (Figure 6.3). Carson, a suburban city dating from the 1960s, has long been popular with Filipinos, especially those leaving the navy-based community in west Long Beach in search of newer homes. A similar expansion of an earlier enclave occurred in the Eagle Rock section of L.A. City and in adjacent Glendale. And in the central San Fernando Valley, the Filipino settlement focus in Panorama City originated with health professional employment in the local Kaiser hospital.

Particularly important was the growth of the large Filipino settlement in upscale suburbs like Walnut, Diamond Bar, Cerritos, and the Stevenson Ranch development west of Interstate 5 near Santa Clarita. Movement into the new city of Chino Hills in San Bernardino County has extended the San

Gabriel Valley settlements still farther eastward. Additional Filipino concentrations in San Bernardino County include tracts close to Loma Linda University Medical Center, where health care professionals are employed, and to the west, near Interstate 15, a suburban tract of newer homes in Fontana.

Filipinos dispersed in older and newer suburbs. The majority of Filipinos in Southern California do not live in ethnic enclaves (Figure 6.3; Table 6.2). Partly because most Filipino immigrants enter with advanced English-language skills and earn the incomes of professionals, most have less need to settle in enclaves. The result is that Filipinos are neighbors of Southern Californians in a wide range of suburban areas.

Chinese

Only a small proportion of Chinese in Southern California as of 2000 are descendants of immigrants who arrived in the United States in the nineteenth century. At that time and up until after World War II, most Chinese who were not servants of White people could not rent an apartment or buy a home in most parts of Los Angeles. Chinese generally had to live in restricted areas, the largest and best known of which were called Chinatowns.

Chinatown and vicinity. There has been a sequence of Chinatowns in different locations near Downtown Los Angeles. All have been east and south of the original Plaza until the 1930s, when Chinatown was established in its present location—just north of the Plaza. Relocation was necessary because the new Union Station was planned for the area in which many Chinese lived. The new Chinatown was planned as a focus for tourism in addition to homes for Chinese.

Shopping arcade, Chinatown

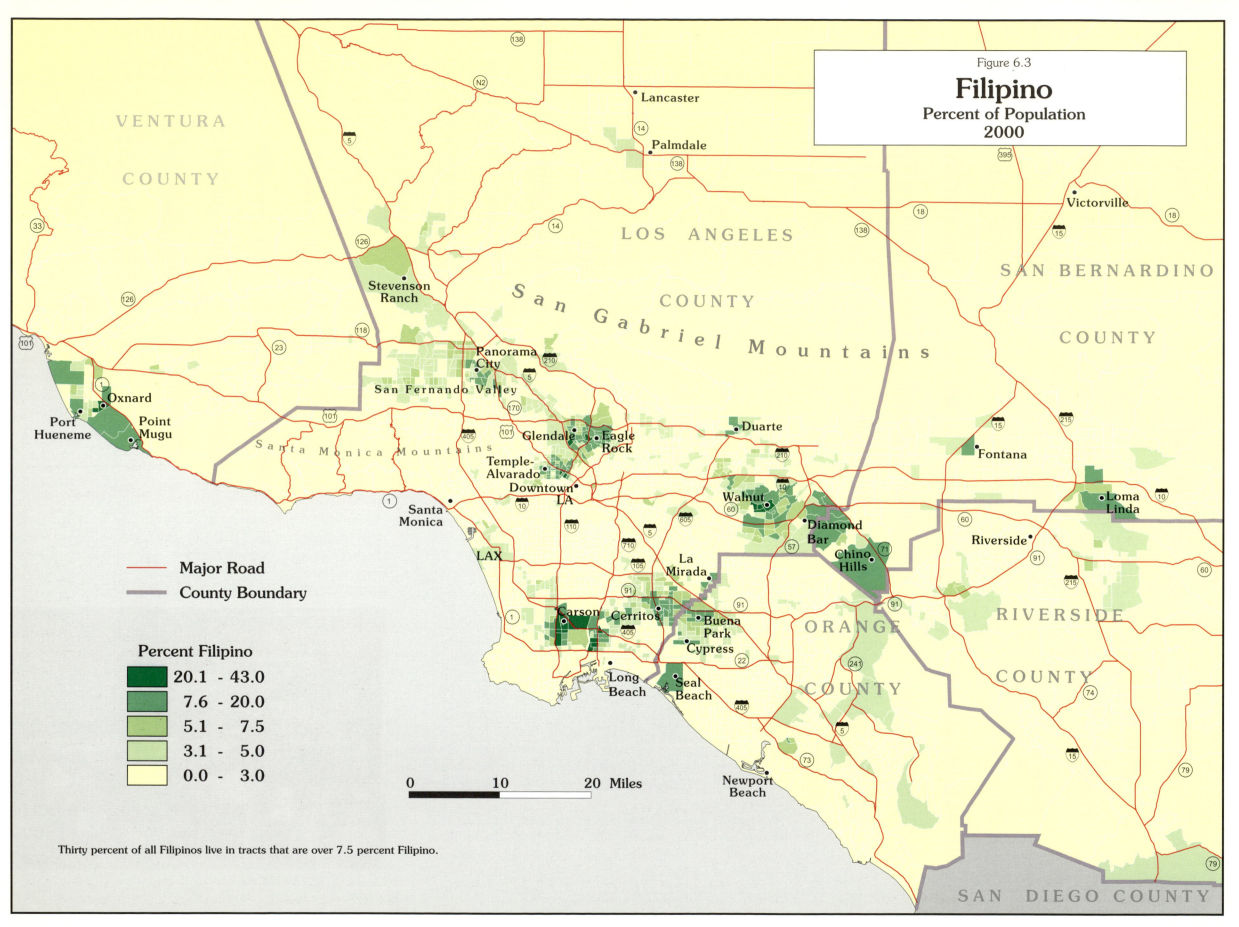

Figure 6.3

Filipino
Percent of Population
2000

Major Road
County Boundary

Percent Filipino
20.1 - 43.0
7.6 - 20.0
5.1 - 7.5
3.1 - 5.0
0.0 - 3.0

0   10   20 Miles

Thirty percent of all Filipinos live in tracts that are over 7.5 percent Filipino.

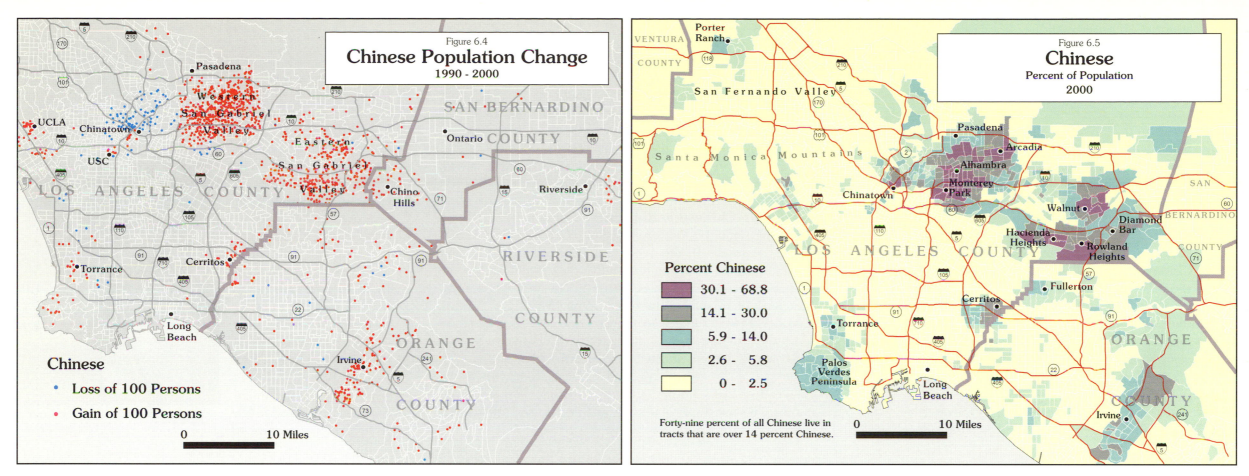

Figure 6.4
Chinese Population Change
1990 - 2000

Chinese
- Loss of 100 Persons
- Gain of 100 Persons

0   10 Miles

Figure 6.5
Chinese
Percent of Population
2000

Percent Chinese
- 30.1 - 68.8
- 14.1 - 30.0
- 5.9 - 14.0
- 2.6 - 5.8
- 0 - 2.5

Forty-nine percent of all Chinese live in tracts that are over 14 percent Chinese.

0   10 Miles

In the 1960s, however, residential shifts began to take place. Many more immigrants began to arrive near the end of that decade, and at the same time residential restrictions on Chinese became much weaker. As a result, Chinese expanded into surrounding neighborhoods. The numbers of Chinese in and near Chinatown grew through the 1980s despite the fact that the area has remained poor and not attractive to most modern-day Chinese immigrants.

During the 1990s, however, resident Chinese tended to leave the older areas that lie within a mile or two of Chinatown but not in its commercial center (Figure 6.4). This change is presumably related to a diminishing number of poor Chinese immigrants and the ability of those already in the area to afford better housing elsewhere. The same out-movement has characterized other low-rent areas to the west, between Downtown and Vermont Avenue, where poor Mexican and Central American immigrants have been eager to live. Because Latino immigrants have far outnumbered Chinese in the entire area north and west of Downtown, shifts in the ethnic composition of such neighborhoods apparently resulted from changes in the relative size and economic status of ethnic populations desiring housing in this area.

In the heart of Chinatown, however, there was a slight decrease in the Chinese population but an increase in the total

Asian population (Figures 6.1, 6.4). This discrepancy is explained by the differing nature of the Asian and Chinese data. The Asian map represents all Asians, with mixed-race Asians fractionally assigned (explained in chapter 2). The Chinese maps are based on those people who reported "Chinese" or "Taiwanese" as their only race on their census questionnaires. Using only this group undercounts Chinese because it excludes mixed-race Chinese, many ethnic Chinese from Southeast Asia, and the many Asians other than Chinese living in Chinatown.[8]

In contrast to the Chinese out-movement from most neighborhoods near Chinatown, in the Los Angeles Downtown itself several hundred older Chinese moved into the attractive Angelus Plaza apartments on the edge of Bunker Hill (Figure 6.4). In those apartment buildings, completed in 1981, rents for low-income seniors are subsidized by the government, making them attractive for poorer Chinese.

The San Gabriel Valley. The largest enclave is in the western San Gabriel Valley (Figure 6.5), where in the 1970s a Chinese developer advertised Monterey Park among Chinese in Taiwan and Hong Kong as "the Chinese Beverly Hills." As a result, many Chinese immigrants settled in Monterey Park and the nearby cities of Alhambra and Rosemead. In the 1980s this

enclave expanded into nearby cities, including more expensive ones like Arcadia and San Marino. Other immigrants headed several miles eastward in the San Gabriel Valley to Walnut, Diamond Bar, and Hacienda Heights, where a large, active Taiwanese Buddhist temple is located. This Eastern San Gabriel Valley area is called the "Eastern District" by many Chinese.

Chief financial officer, East-West Bank, San Marino

Chinese settlement in the western and eastern San Gabriel Valley can be thought of as a single ethnic suburban enclave that integrates residential areas with a great range of Chinese businesses and professional services, making immigrants feel particularly at home.[9] This "ethnoburb" is home to Chinese from over thirty different countries or overseas areas. It is probably the single most important center in this country for international transactions and linkages between the United States and the Chinese in China, the special area of Hong Kong, Taiwan, and Southeast Asia. The Chinese presence in the San Gabriel Valley illustrates vividly the local expression of globalization in its cultural, social, and economic dimensions.

Within the Valley, there is some spatial patterning of Chinese according to their various countries of origin. However, the residential pattern is primarily due to their varying levels of education, income, and wealth. Because the more affluent immigrants tend to be from Hong Kong and Taiwan, people from these origins predominate in the more expensive areas like Arcadia, San Marino, and the newer neighborhoods of the eastern San Gabriel Valley. At the other extreme, Chinese from Southeast Asia, primarily Vietnam and Cambodia, immigrated with the least money and skills. They are thus better represented in areas with lower-cost housing, such as El Monte, La Puente, and the City of Industry.

The western and eastern sections of the Chinese settlement in the San Gabriel Valley are separated by industrial areas and poorer and predominantly Latino neighborhoods. While there is some residential mixing, there is a greater tendency for Chinese and Latinos to occupy different neighborhoods, usually defined by differences in housing costs.

During the 1990s, the San Gabriel Valley became even more strongly Chinese, as this group occupied the former homes and apartments of Whites and Latinos. The Hispanic change map shows this clearly in the decrease of Latinos in Monterey Park (Figure 5.1). On the Chinese change map (Figure 6.4), the eastern boundary of Los Angeles City marks a divide between areas of Chinese population increase and decrease. There has been a net out-movement of Chinese from Los Angeles, in part a response to problems in the Los Angeles Unified School District. In contrast, Chinese numbers in Alhambra, South Pasadena, San Gabriel, El Monte, Temple City, Arcadia, and San Marino continued to grow during the 1990s.

Other Chinese settlements. Beginning in the 1970s many more affluent Chinese moved into Cerritos and the Palos Verdes Peninsula. In the 1980s and 1990 others bought new homes in the northern San Fernando Valley. Irvine has become an important Asian enclave, with Chinese well represented. Just north of Route 73 (the San Joaquin Hills Transportation Corridor) the tract indicated as over 14-percent Chinese represents the campus of the University of California at Irvine, where most Chinese are students in dormitories (Figure 6.5). There are also growing clusters of Chinese students near the campuses of USC, UCLA, and UC Riverside. Not shown on our maps is some dispersal into Thousand Oaks and other newer suburbs of eastern Ventura County.

Japanese

Japanese first settled in Southern California about a hundred years ago, arriving about thirty years after the Chinese. Immigrants in both groups were typically laborers at first, but because Japanese laborers were permitted to bring in "picture brides" from Japan as wives, the Japanese formed families and more stable communities than did the early Chinese. During the last thirty years, Chinese immigrants have far outnumbered those from Japan. This is because the economic success of Japan has meant that fewer Japanese have needed to migrate in order to better themselves.

The net effect of these two factors has been that, despite forced removal to internment camps during World War II, a higher percentage of

Little Tokyo

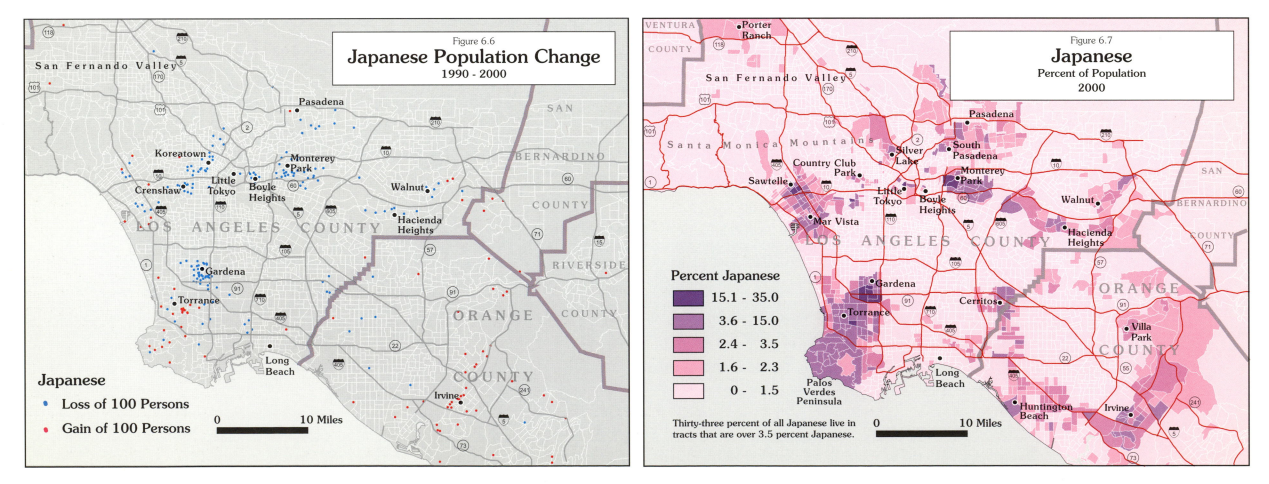

Japanese in Southern California are descendants of pre-World War II Southern California families than is true among the Chinese.[10]

Little Tokyo. The leading Japanese residential and business center, Little Tokyo, emerged in the early twentieth century to the south and east of Downtown L.A. With redevelopment in the 1970s and 1980s, it was modernized. It now contains a variety of shops, restaurants, and hotels serving Los Angeles residents, particularly Japanese, and tourists and businessmen from Japan. Although it is more important as a commercial center than a residential area, modern apartment buildings were constructed, and many older Japanese live in Little Tokyo Towers and other housing complexes.

Little Tokyo, with L.A. City Hall

The map of Asian population change during the 1990s (Figure 6.1) shows a gain in Little Tokyo, but the Japanese map indicates no change (Figure 6.6). What appears at first as a discrepancy is really the result of much greater Asian diversity in Little Tokyo and the fact that mixed-race Japanese could not be included in the data for the Japanese change map. In the single tract that covers Little Tokyo over one-third of its Asians were not Japanese.[11]

Weakening of some enclaves in older suburbs. During the 1990s Japanese continued to leave the old Japanese neighborhoods in Hollywood and Boyle Heights, where Japanese families had made their homes prior to 1925. Occasionally one sees remnants in the landscape of these old Japanese settlements, the most noticeable of which are the thriving Tenriko Church and Nichiren Buddhist Temple in Boyle Heights.

In the neighborhoods near the intersection of Crenshaw and Jefferson Blvds., about three miles west of Downtown, a similar out-movement has taken place. Japanese first settled this area in the 1940s, before and after their internment in the camps. But in the 1950s and 1960s Japanese began to leave, attracted by the newer homes being built in the Gardena area which they were then permitted to buy or rent. The death of older Japanese and the departure of others from the Crenshaw area has continued to weaken the Japanese presence there.

Many Japanese have also left the older post-World War II suburbs—Gardena and Monterey Park—in which they had been prominent settlers. Gardena had been a Japanese farming community, which dated from the first decade of the twentieth century. This made it particularly attractive to Japanese families during suburban development in the 1950s. In Monterey Park, Japanese families who moved into the new homes after World War II found much initial resistance by Whites but ultimately felt accepted because they were "good neighbors".[12] Although many subsequently sold their homes to eager Chinese immigrants, Monterey Park remains an important Japanese enclave (Figure 6.7).

Strengthening of older suburban enclaves. Between the Pacific Ocean and Interstate 405, the Sawtelle and Mar Vista-Culver City areas, where Japanese settlement dates from before World War II, continue as important centers. There is also a thriving Japanese shopping district along Sawtelle Blvd. in West Los Angeles. The resilience of this enclave may be related to continuing investment by ethnic businesses.

The Gardena-Torrance area, including the Palos Verdes Peninsula, remains the largest Japanese enclave in Southern California (Figure 6.7). It has long been a home for U.S.-born Japanese, most of whom are third- or fourth-generation Americans. The enclave also contains many immigrants and temporary visitors from Japan, including Japanese nationals assigned temporarily by their companies to Southern California. The net movement of Japanese into Torrance and nearby cities during the 1990s tended to sustain property values and accentuate its ethnic identity (Figure 6.6).

Japanese have been moving into many of the same upscale newer suburbs with good schools that have attracted other Asians and Whites: Diamond Bar and Hacienda Heights, Cerritos, Irvine, and other newer sections of Orange County. In Pomona, the tract that is between 3 and 15 percent Japanese is the campus of Cal Poly Pomona (California State Polytechnic University), where many Japanese students live in dorms.

Dispersal from enclaves. Since the return of many Japanese in the late 1940s after internment, residential shifts have tended toward dispersal from former enclaves. Although

this text has focused on Japanese enclaves, by 2000 only a third of the Japanese in Southern California lived in neighborhoods that were over 3.5 percent Japanese (Figure 6.7). Without the evidence from the map, Southern Californians might not be aware of the many Los Angeles or Orange County neighborhoods where Japanese comprise only a very small proportion of the residents. Most of these dispersed Japanese are the completely Americanized U.S.-born children, grandchildren, and great-grandchildren of immigrants.

Koreans

Koreatown. The most important Korean enclave in Los Angeles is Koreatown, where over 40,000 Koreans live. This area is best known for its Korean businesses—ranging from clothing and shoe stores to coffee shops, restaurants, travel agencies, banks, law firms, and doctors offices. With the great popularity of golf among Korean immigrants, there are also several driving ranges, visible as large netted cages. Koreatown's businesses serve mostly neighborhood Koreans and the larger Korean community of Southern California.

Koreatown is located in a cultural and economic transition area—between the low-rent and mostly Latino neighborhoods to the east and south and the mostly White and affluent Hancock Park neighborhood to the west (Figures 6.8 and 6.9). Koreans have always represented a minority of the neighborhood residents, who are mixed ethnically but mostly Latino. However, during the 1990s the Korean presence became stronger as many Koreans bought or leased older businesses, restaurants, office buildings, and churches, thus slowly replacing traditional White-controlled institutions.

In the 1990s, the percentage of Koreans in Koreatown also increased—from about 16 percent to over 20 percent. Ten tracts in Koreatown are now over one-third Korean although none has a Korean majority. The growth of the Korean population is probably related to an increase of elderly in nursing homes and other Korean residents in new luxury apartment buildings.[13] Most of these apartment buildings are in an attractive and affluent section of Koreatown north of Wilshire Blvd. that contrasts sharply with some poorer areas in the more southerly portion of Koreatown. In addition, compared to previous decades more Koreans may have been overstaying their student or tourist visas, and Koreatown probably attracts these and other undocumented Koreans because of its many opportunities to work in ethnic businesses.

Korean settlement expanded westward in the 1990s from Koreatown into the Park La Brea area. Some economically successful Koreans moved into the more expensive Country Club Park and Hancock Park neighborhoods, which are over 8 percent Korean. The proximity of those better areas to Koreatown means a much shorter commute to work than would be possible from the suburbs.

The northward shift of Koreatown that occurred during earlier decades has continued, as departure from the southern portion (between Pico Blvd. and San Marino Street) of the traditional Koreatown is clearly evident (Figure 6.8). In the poorer parts of Hollywood, there was also some Korean out-movement. Koreans may have moved out of these areas partly because of the growing numbers of poor people, mostly Latinos.

Korean businesses in South Central. Although few Koreans live in South Central Los Angeles (Figure 6.9), many own businesses there. Since the early 1970s, Koreans have been more likely than the average immigrant to buy retail businesses or develop their own new business. Those who lacked enough capital to buy in the suburbs frequently bought grocery or liquor stores in poorer parts of Los Angeles, often in South Central. Their patrons were neighborhood residents, usually Blacks or, increasingly, Latinos.

Prior to the 1992 riot that was triggered by the acquittal of the police officers in the Rodney King beating case, cultural and economic differences between Korean merchants and Black customers made for much suspicion and resentment between the two groups. In the destruction that followed, many of the businesses that were burned were Korean-owned. For many Korean merchants the riots were devastating. Some moved temporarily away, but most eventually returned to Los Angeles.[14] By 2000 several hundred Korean grocers were again doing business in South Central Los Angeles.[15] The widespread availability of liquor in South Central has been a related issue. Many Koreans who owned liquor stores that were destroyed in the riots did not rebuild, a leading factor in reducing by 20 percent the number of stores in South Central selling liquor.[16]

The riot also prompted many Koreans who remained in business to rethink their earlier aloofness regarding both their customers and the larger American society. Many Koreans resolved to play more active roles in the political process.[17] Korean merchants appear to be showing a new respect for and friendly treatment of their Black and Latino customers. However, most Korean merchants still feel stressed by cultural tensions with their clientele.[18]

Suburban enclaves. The most significant residential shifts during the 1990s involved departures from older, poorer areas and settlement in more affluent areas, often leading to growing concentrations of Koreans (Figure 6.8). In earlier decades Koreans had followed Japanese suburbanites into the once-rural historic Japanese settlement of Gardena. However, in the 1990s many Koreans, like many Japanese, moved out of their modest apartments and homes in Gardena. Koreans also left ethnically mixed areas of Hollywood and Arleta in the San Fernando Valley. On the other hand, Korean population increases occurred in many of the same areas where other Asians live—Hacienda Heights, Diamond Bar, Cerritos, Irvine, and the Torrance-Palos Verdes Peninsula area. The net effect is a clearly growing set of Asian ethnic communities in some of the more attractive suburban cities of Southern California (Figure 6.9).

Some other Asian suburban settlements are mostly Korean. This is the case in Glendale, where many Koreans have upscale homes in the hilly southeastern section of the city. The enclave continues to the north, in the valley between the Verdugo and San Gabriel Mountains, in cities like La Cañada-Flintridge. In the San Fernando Valley, the recently developed Porter Ranch area of Northridge and adjacent Granada Hills have become a residential focus for more affluent Koreans. In Orange County, Garden Grove has a major Korean settlement, and the enclave in Fullerton has expanded geographically into Buena Park and across the county line into La Mirada.

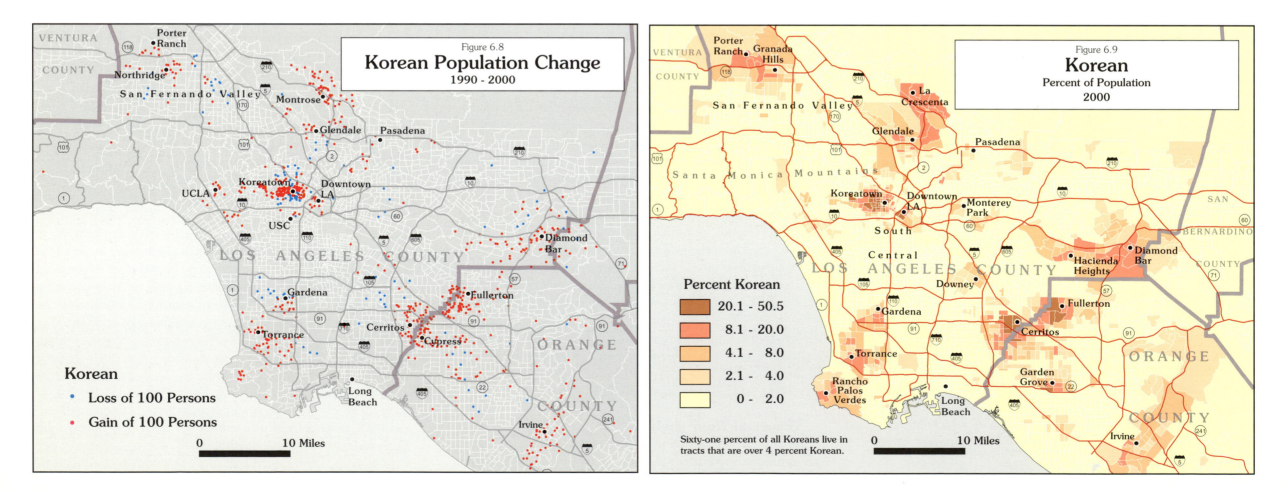

Figure 6.8
Korean Population Change
1990 - 2000

Korean
• Loss of 100 Persons
• Gain of 100 Persons

0   10 Miles

Figure 6.9
Korean
Percent of Population
2000

Percent Korean
20.1 - 50.5
8.1 - 20.0
4.1 - 8.0
2.1 - 4.0
0 - 2.0

Sixty-one percent of all Koreans live in tracts that are over 4 percent Korean.

0   10 Miles

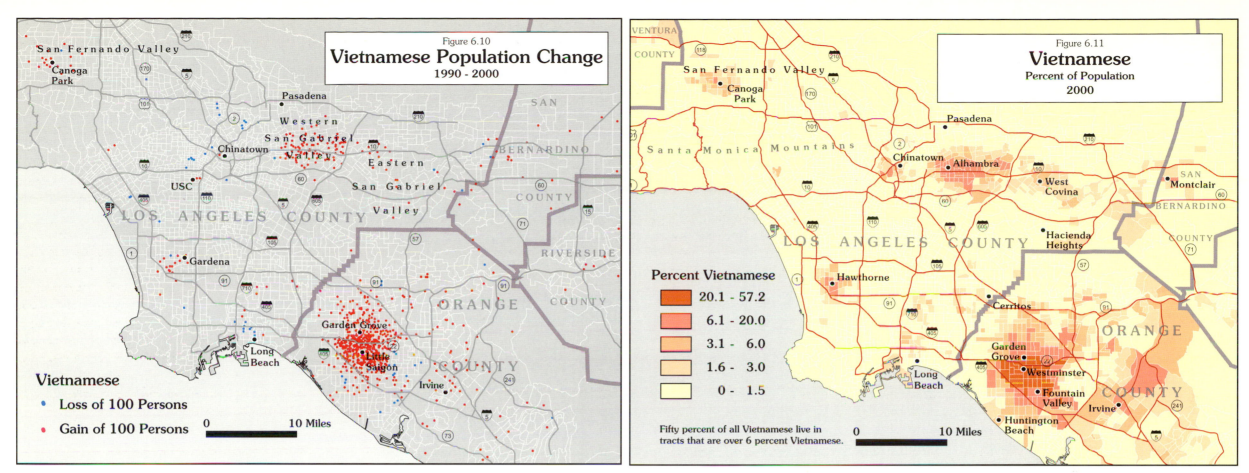

Figure 6.10
Vietnamese Population Change
1990 - 2000

Vietnamese
• Loss of 100 Persons
• Gain of 100 Persons
0   10 Miles

Figure 6.11
Vietnamese
Percent of Population
2000

Percent Vietnamese
20.1 - 57.2
6.1 - 20.0
3.1 - 6.0
1.6 - 3.0
0 - 1.5

Fifty percent of all Vietnamese live in tracts that are over 6 percent Vietnamese.
0   10 Miles

Vietnamese

Nearly all the first Vietnamese in Southern California arrived as refugees beginning in 1975. The initial group was evacuated from Saigon in late April, when the Americans and South Vietnamese were defeated by the communist forces based in the north.

Little Saigon. Many in this first wave of refugees were processed through the Camp Pendleton Marine base just south of Orange County. Voluntary refugee agencies arranged American sponsors for refugee families in many parts of the United States, but in Orange County so many churches and other organizations offered to sponsor families that Orange County immediately received a large Vietnamese population.

In the late 1970s and early 1980s the many Vietnamese who had been scattered across the country struggled to adapt to American society and its economy. However, most Vietnamese in such places felt isolated, and many migrated to be closer to members of their extended families and other Vietnamese. Orange County was one place that attracted many migrants from other states. By 1990 it held the largest Vietnamese population in the United States.

Orange County's older suburban cities had apartments and houses that were not too expensive, as well as jobs in nearby electronics assembly (Figure 6.11). Bolsa Avenue in the city of Westminster and adjacent sections of Garden Grove were slowly built up with new Vietnamese shopping centers. These contained numerous restaurants and noodle houses and bakeries, doctors' and lawyers' offices, grocery and shoe stores, and travel agents—all patronized by the Vietnamese community. Later this growing concentration became the place of publication for several Vietnamese newspapers and magazines as well as the center for Vietnamese television, video, and radio production.[19] Vietnamese have kept the area as attractive and safe as possible because it symbolizes their community to themselves, to non-resident Vietnamese, and to other Americans.

The enclave became widely known as Little Saigon. Whereas the city of Saigon in Vietnam was renamed "Ho Chi Minh City" in 1975 in honor of that communist Vietnamese leader, in Orange County the name "Little Saigon" reminds everyone of the pre-communist period and the strongly held anti-communist views of local Vietnamese community leaders.

During the 1990s the number of Vietnamese in Orange County doubled because of the arrival of new immigrants from Vietnam and a high birthrate among earlier arrivals (Figure 6.10). The stores of Little Saigon now sell everything from handmade artwork, silk, and clothing for the fashion-conscious consumer to Asian herbs, fresh seafood, books, and Vietnamese music CDs.[20] Some of the many restaurants show the influence of French cooking from the colonial past, and others specialize in Vietnamese regional cuisine. Residentially, the enclave has expanded into parts of several cities—Fountain Valley, Tustin, Huntington Beach, and Santa Ana. In 2000 Vietnamese comprised half the residents of some neighborhoods in the extended Little Saigon area (Figure 6.11).

The net migration of Vietnamese into Orange County from other parts of the country that characterized the 1980s stopped in the 1990s. Thus, Vietnamese in America became more settled. Orange County in 2000 was home to about 12 percent of Vietnamese in the U.S., the same as 1990.

Other enclaves. Nationally, the second most important Vietnamese concentration is in the San Jose (Silicon Valley) area, where many Vietnamese have worked in electronics and as assemblers of computer equipment. Los Angeles County has the third largest Vietnamese population, although growth here during the 1990s was not as rapid as in many other places.

The largest Vietnamese enclave in Los Angeles County is in Monterey Park, where most of the Vietnamese represented on the map are ethnically Chinese. Linguistically, however, many speak Vietnamese, which explains why business signs in the Vietnamese language are common. Because their families had lived for some generations in Vietnam, many of these Chinese-Vietnamese identified themselves as Vietnamese on the census questionnaire and thus appear on this map.

In any walk through Los Angeles' Chinatown, particularly its busy southern half, one may observe numerous small shops and professional services run by Chinese-Vietnamese. Many of these businesses are in multistory arcades built in the late 1980s and 1990s with multilingual signs in Chinese, Vietnamese, and other languages. Although some of these Vietnamese-Chinese live in Chinatown (Figure 6.11), probably most business owners and many of their workers live a few miles to the east in Monterey Park or nearby areas.

Local changes. The 1990s pattern of Vietnamese residential shifts in Southern California has been mixed (Figure 6.10). There has been some movement out of poorer areas, such as Santa Ana and Long Beach, and movement somewhat closer toward larger Vietnamese neighborhoods. This occurred in the West San Fernando Valley, the Gardena-Hawthorne area, and the San Gabriel Valley. At the same time, Vietnamese have increased in numbers a few miles away from their major concentrations, perhaps because of dispersal into better neighborhoods from which the familiar churches, temples, grocery stores, etc. are still easily reached by car. Thus, Vietnamese have moved to Diamond Bar and Chino Hills. Similarly, in Orange County there has been some dispersal into more expensive homes of Irvine and central and southern Orange County.

Jeweler, Little Saigon

Asian Settlement in Enclaves and Changes

The summary distribution of Asians clearly indicates their importance in some areas of Southern California (Figure 6.12). Census tracts that are over 40 percent Asian indicate particularly significant concentrations. The two largest enclaves are in the Monterey Park area of the western San Gabriel Valley and in Walnut, Rowland Heights, and nearby places in the eastern San Gabriel Valley. The separate Asian settlements in Cerritos

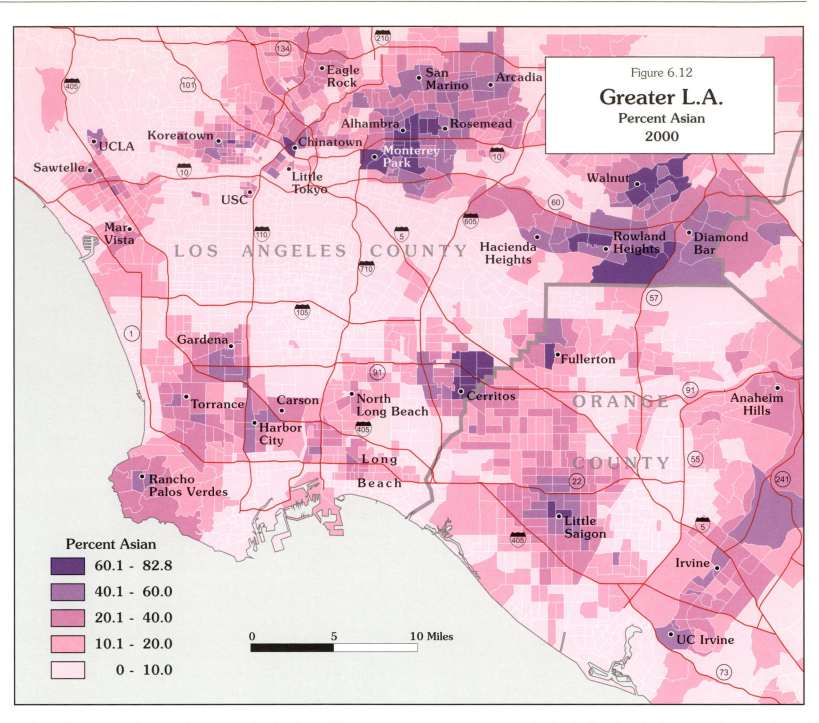

Figure 6.12

Greater L.A.
Percent Asian
2000

Percent Asian
- 60.1 – 82.8
- 40.1 – 60.0
- 20.1 – 40.0
- 10.1 – 20.0
- 0 – 10.0

0   5   10 Miles

and Little Saigon also stand out—as do Gardena, Torrance, Irvine, Chinatown, and Koreatown to a lesser extent. Asian students in dormitories or nearby apartments are evident at campuses of the University of California at Los Angeles (UCLA) and at Irvine (UCI), as well as at the University of Southern California (USC).

During the 1990s Asians tended to settle among other Asians (Table 6.2). In 2000 over 30 percent of Asians in Southern California lived in census tracts that were over one-third Asian. This trend toward increasing ethnic concentration

is consistent with the higher level of Asian-White residential separation as measured over the same decade (Table 7.2).

In 1990 Filipinos and Japanese were the two Asian groups least likely to be living in enclaves. This should be directly related to higher levels of assimilation to mainstream American culture, indicated by their higher proportions of people who speak English only or very well.[21] The trends of these groups diverged during the 1990s, for reasons that are unknown to us. Filipinos became the only large Asian group that decreased its residential concentration while Japanese tended to relocate toward

Table 6.2. Enclave Settlement of Asian Groups, 1990 and 2000: Los Angeles CMSA

Group	Threshold for Enclaves		Percent in Enclaves		Change 1990-2000
	1990	2000	1990	2000	
Asian Total	27.6	33.7	26.1	30.9	+6.1
Filipino	6.0	6.8	36.9	31.9	-5.0
Chinese	6.3	7.6	51.2	60.1	+8.9
Japanese	3.6	2.9	35.2	39.0	+3.8
Korean	4.0	4.7	47.7	56.1	+8.4
Vietnamese	3.1	4.3	50.1	57.2	+7.1

Sources: 1990 U.S. Census STF1; Census 2000 race tables.

Notes: Ethnic enclaves are all census tracts in which the group is represented at more than three times their percentage of the total population, as explained in chapter 1. Threshold values are the lowest percentage values that define enclave settlement for any group and year. Thresholds and percentages for the Asian total include fractionally assigned mixed-race Asians, but calculations for specific groups are based on those reporting only a single race.

Japanese enclaves. The other Asian groups clearly increased in proportions living in enclaves despite the higher threshold value defining enclaves as of 2000.

Traditional understanding of enclaves. In the United States, according to both immigrant spatial assimilation theory and empirical research, residents of ethnic enclaves have had lower levels of income and cultural assimilation than members of the same group living outside such enclaves.[22] As immigrants or ethnic groups assimilate culturally and economically, they should leave enclaves. Over the long run, enclaves for any ethnic group should diminish, particularly in today's world where people can so easily stay in touch through telephones, email, and automobiles.[23]

New phenomenon of higher-status enclaves. The cultural dimension of Asian enclaves seems consistent with the traditional theory of immigrant spatial assimilation. Living in an enclave probably still enhances immigrants' cultural comfort and convenience to ethnic stores and institutions.[24] Thus, the overall growth of Asian enclaves during the 1990s in the Los Angeles CMSA can probably be explained by the 45-percent growth in the number of people born in Asian countries, the 39-percent increase of number of speakers of Asian and Pacific languages, and the 10-percent increase in the speakers of those languages who did not speak English very well.[25]

However, the relatively high economic status of most Asian enclaves is unexpected. Most Asian enclaves in Southern California are not the poor areas consistent with traditional theory. Our description in this chapter of Asian enclaves as middle- and upper-income areas has been confirmed for 1990 by

Hum and Zonta.[26] According to their research, Asian professionals, executives, and managers in Los Angeles County were as likely to settle in enclaves as were those in low-skilled occupations, although the two different occupational groups tended to settle in different enclaves. Higher-status enclaves attracted 42 percent of new Asian immigrants who worked in professional positions. In addition, findings by other researchers demonstrate that residents of Asian enclaves in Los Angeles County did have much higher incomes than average as of 1990.[27]

Whereas traditional lower-status enclaves developed under conditions of cultural and financial constraints, the higher-status enclaves seem to result from voluntary spatial concentration made possible by the more-than-adequate financial resources of many Asian immigrants. Most Asians, including the many who arrived during the 1990s, can afford a wide range of places within Southern California. Their choice of an enclave residential location must reflect their preference for this, presumably for the traditional reasons of cultural comfort and convenience to ethnic resources.

It is significant that different Asian groups have often moved into the same enclaves. These multiethnic Asian enclaves are attractive suburban areas with good schools. It is likely that this residential proximity, reflecting shared values and income levels, will promote mutual support among the different groups and a shared identity as Asian Americans.

Notes

1. Allen and Turner (1997), 249.
2. Allen and Turner (1996b); Massey (1985).
3. Cleeland (1998).
4. Kotkin (2000), 39.
5. Quinsaat (1976).
6. Triem (1985), 130.
7. Shulman (2001).
8. The composition of the Asian population in Los Angeles' Chinatown (tract 2071) in 2000 was as follows: A total of 3,944 individuals identified only as Chinese. An additional 136 persons reported themselves as both Chinese and another Asian race, mostly Chinese-Vietnamese and Chinese-Cambodian. Another 37 were Chinese mixed with some non-Asian race, most likely White. Completely separate residents in the same tract were the following Asians who reported themselves by only a single race: 337 Vietnamese, 110 Cambodians, 19 Filipinos, 17 Japanese, 17 Asian Indians, 16 Koreans, 16 Thais, and 29 other Asians.
9. The description of this Chinese "ethnoburb" is based primarily on Li (1998). The various factors leading to the development of the large Chinese enclave in Monterey Park and the San Gabriel Valley are thoroughly explained in Li (1999). Also, Monterey Park has been much studied as a testing ground for interethnic relations, socially and politically. Two recent studies that cover that body of research are Fong (2001) and Saito (2001).

10. The extent to which old Japanese communities persist today depends on their pre-World War II size and changes since that War. Los Angeles and the agriculture-based Japanese settlements in the Gardena-Long Beach area and Orange County have had viable Japanese communities for over eighty years. Because the former Japanese settlements of Riverside and Oxnard were smaller, only a few current residents of those areas are likely to be descendants of the old pioneering families.
11. In addition to the 657 residents of Little Tokyo (tract 2062) who checked only Japanese on the census questionnaire, 188 Koreans, 77 Chinese, 26 Thais, 21 Filipinos, 10 Lao, 5 Vietnamese, 4 Sri Lankans, 3 Asian Indians, 2 Indonesians, and 1 Cambodian were counted. Also, 35 others marked two Asian race categories, and another 57 identified themselves racially as both Asian and non-Asian.
12. Saito (2001).
13. Edward J. W. Park of Loyola Marymount University suggested these explanations of the growth of the Korean population in Koreatown.
14. Charles Kim, Executive Director of the Korean American Coalition, interviewed March 2002.
15. Kang (2000).
16. Robinson-Jacobs (2002). According to Charles Kim, the strong opposition of Black community leaders to the proliferation of liquor stores in South Central expressed through the requirement to obtain a new conditional-use permit was the main factor in the decision by many Koreans not to return to that business in South Central.
17. Park (2001).
18. Kang and Richardson (2002).
19. Freeman (1995).
20. Letran (2000).
21. Allen and Turner (1997), 238.
22. Allen and Turner (1996b); Massey (1985). Cultural assimilation is most commonly measured by English-language skill.
23. Zelinsky and Lee (1998).
24. Kempen and Ozuekren (1998).
25. U.S. Census Bureau (1993d), Tables 27, 28; U.S. Census Bureau (2002c), Table DP-2. The much greater preference for living in enclaves on the part of foreign-born Asians compared to U.S.-born Asians in Los Angeles County was demonstrated in survey results from the early 1990s (Charles 2001), 265.
26. Hum and Zonta (2000).
27. Because Census 2000 data on income and occupation are not yet available, we use calculations by Logan, Alba, and Zhang (2002) for 1990 to show that residents of most Asian enclaves in Los Angeles County had income levels substantially above average. The median income of all households in Los Angeles County in 1990 was $34,965 (U.S. Census Bureau 1993b). Listed below for each group are the median incomes of households in enclaves within Los Angeles County but outside Los Angeles City, as reported by Logan, Alba, and Zhang (2002), 314-315. Chinese - $43,601; Filipinos - $45,628; Japanese - $46,626; Koreans - $49,432; Vietnamese - $37,885. Thus, only Vietnamese households had a median income close to the county average.

7. General Patterns

In this chapter we synthesize some of the larger distributions from the maps of specific ethnic groups. First is a summary map that identifies by color the predominant or numerically largest ethnic group in each census tract (Figure 7.1). Next, we focus on ethnic diversity and mixing. Tracts in which Whites, Blacks, Latinos, and Asians are somewhat evenly mixed are considered highly diverse whereas other tracts that have high proportions of just one or two ethnic groups and very few members of the other groups are not diverse (Figure 7.2). We also look at the completely new multiracial data from Census 2000 and examine variations in proportions of tract residents who identified themselves as having more than one race (Figure 7.3).

These maps plus those presented in previous chapters allow one to see both the general pattern of group distributions and the details of ethnic settlement in specific neighborhoods. Nevertheless, the maps are too detailed to permit quick summaries of comparative distributions and their trends.

To obtain convenient summaries of the patterns, we introduce in the third section a statistic that has been widely used in the social sciences for this purpose. This statistic—the index of dissimilarity—measures the level of residential segregation or spatial separation between two groups. However, the word "segregation" conveys a powerfully negative connotation that was appropriate to the blatant and rigid racism of three or more decades ago. At that time Whites attempted to enforce residential segregation on minority peoples, and Blacks were often described as living in ghettoes because they were not permitted to move into White neighborhoods. Although some maps show a few effects of those days, in the last thirty years the social situation has become much more open and fluid. Today, "segregation" seems an unduly harsh term for describing modern patterns of group spatial distinctiveness in Southern California. For this reason, we have substituted the milder term "separation," meaning spatial or geographical separation, for what other scholars have called "segregation."

Predominant Ethnic Group

The residential patterns of Whites, Latinos, Blacks, and Asians can be synthesized and summarized in a single map (Figure 7.1). The color conveys the numerically largest group in each tract, and the shade of the color identifies the proportional strength of that group.

Very evident is the large portion of Southern California in which the largest group represents over 70 percent of the total population. This indicates the importance of ethnic differences from place to place. It confirms our belief that the ethnic character of Southern California is impossible to understand without examining it geographically.

Latinos and Whites. In 2000 Whites and Latinos were almost equal in population: 6.5 million Whites and 6.6 million Latinos. Despite similar numbers, the large areas of the map shown in green reflect White predominance in both the more expensive, low-density outer suburbs and large tracts in mountain areas, where there are few residents. In contrast, most of the Latino-plurality tracts are clearly urban and contain higher population densities.

Street fair, MacArthur Park

The most notable exceptions to this are the Santa Clarita Valley towns of Santa Paula, Fillmore, and Piru along Route 126 in Ventura County. This rural area has been home to both Whites and Mexicans, the latter having arrived originally as workers in the citrus orchards and farms. Clearly, Whites who have moved in more recently seeking lower housing prices and scenic amenities have not come in sufficient numbers to change the Latino majorities.

The different locations of White and Latino concentrations result primarily from differences in historical settlement locations and income differences between the two groups. Where White and Latino concentrations occur close together, the two areas differ substantially in housing prices, with Whites occupying the more expensive homes. Such ethnic and economic transitions occur in many places—between mostly White Costa Mesa and Latino Santa Ana, between mostly White Glendora and mostly Latino Azusa, and in Oxnard. Even small areas are explained in the same ways, such as the two Latino pockets in the generally White west San Fernando Valley. In all these places, the situation is likely to result in heightened ethnic-class awareness and tensions.

Baptism, La Placita, L.A. Plaza

Black and Asian enclaves. Figure 7.1 provides the most up-to-date indication of the changing ethnic balance between Blacks and Latinos. It is clear that almost the entire area east of Interstate 110 and north of Interstate 105, including Watts, is predominantly Latino now. To the south, most of

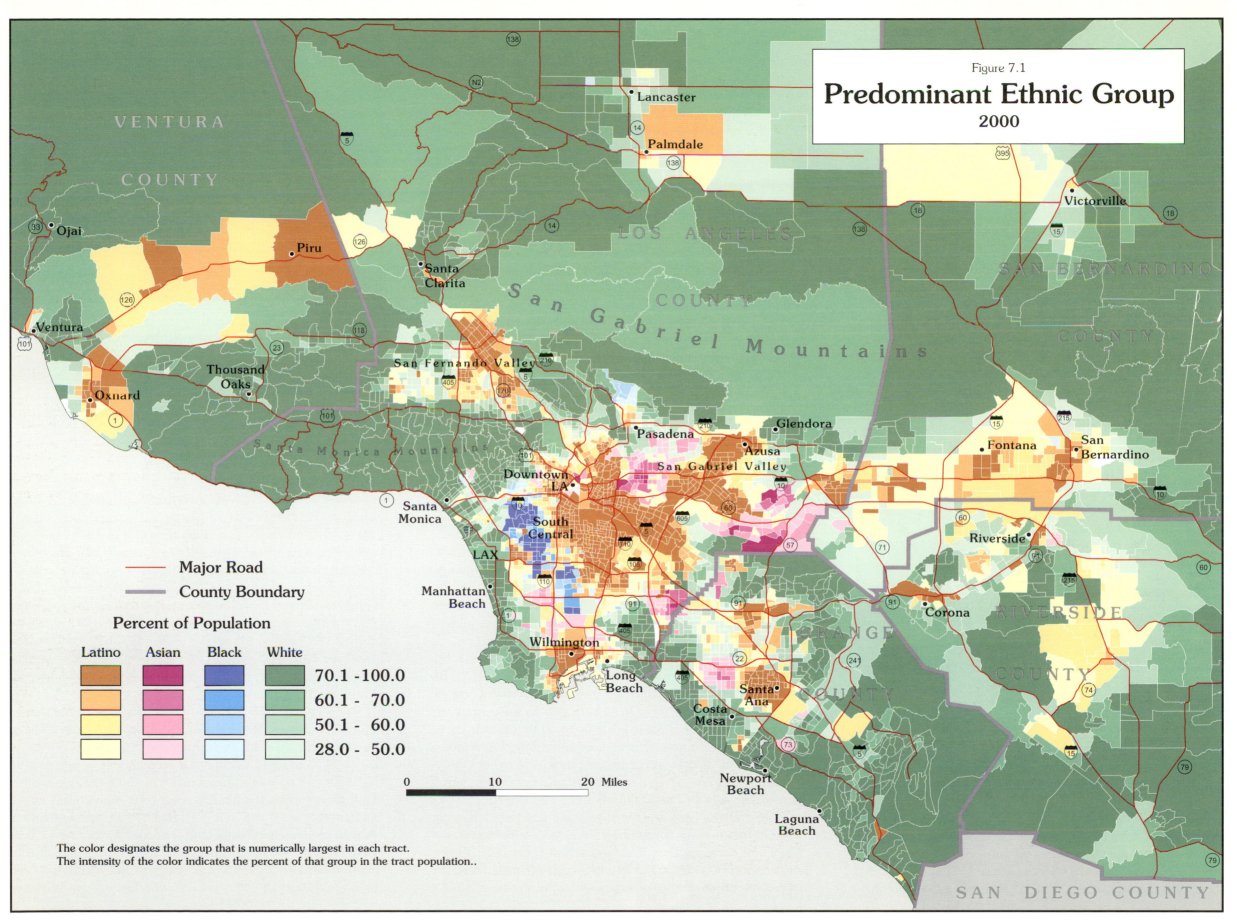

Figure 7.1
Predominant Ethnic Group
2000

Major Road

County Boundary

Percent of Population

Latino	Asian	Black	White	
				70.1 - 100.0
				60.1 - 70.0
				50.1 - 60.0
				28.0 - 50.0

0   10   20 Miles

The color designates the group that is numerically largest in each tract.
The intensity of the color indicates the percent of that group in the tract population..

Willowbrook, western Compton, and northern Carson remain mostly Black. To the west of Interstate 15, Latinos predominate east of Vermont Avenue and in the Lennox area west of Crenshaw Blvd. Although in general the Black enclave remains an area of poverty, on the western side are many middle- or upper-class neighborhoods, home to many leaders of the Black community.

The situation of older Asian enclaves depends on the relative numbers of other groups settling in the area. Most tracts in Koreatown have Latino pluralities because most Koreans live in the suburbs. However, enough Chinese and other Asians have continued to live in Chinatown so that its major tract is over 70 percent Asian.

Most of the larger Asian enclaves were established after 1970, many in affluent neighborhoods. These include the large enclaves of Vietnamese in Little Saigon and Chinese in Monterey Park, as well as multiethnic Asian enclaves in Cerritos and the east San Gabriel Valley. Enclaves originating after 1970 cannot be explained by residential restrictions prior to the 1960s, and the higher-status enclaves appear to result from voluntary choice on the part of many Asians.

Alvarado Street, Pico-Union

Ethnic Diversity

With greatly increased immigration from many different countries and cultures since about 1970, Southern California has become much more ethnically diverse. Everyone is aware of this increased diversity. Many people extol the virtues of this diversity—its stimulating effects on culture and the economy and its jarring of Southern Californians out of traditional attitudes of ethnocentric complacency. Many others point to prob-

lems represented by the many languages spoken, culture conflicts, and frequently divided loyalties between countries of former residence and the United States. In this book we do not attempt to assess the contributions of this diversity.

We do, however, measure and map this diversity as an indication of the varied levels of residential mixing found in different neighborhoods.[1] Because Southern California as a whole is becoming more diverse, studying contemporary ethnic group relationships in those localities that are most diverse can give indications as to how increasing diversity is likely to play out elsewhere in the region.

Diversity is usually measured by the entropy index (also called the diversity index), which summarizes the relative evenness in proportion of different ethnic groups in any area.[2] For Figure 7.2 we calculated diversity in terms of the four largest ethnic groups: non-Hispanic Whites, non-Hispanic Blacks, non-Hispanic Asians, and Latinos. Although American Indians are also one of the basic ethnic categories in the census, they are so much smaller in numbers and so highly dispersed that we did not include them in calculating diversity.

The lowest possible diversity, with a value of 0, occurs when only one group is represented in a census tract. Because calculations of the index frequently exceed 1 in high-diversity areas, we have proportionately normalized the values. Normalization assigns a value of 1 to perfect diversity, in which the four groups are equally represented. The relative diversity of a tract can then be more easily understood in comparison to a situation of maximum possible diversity.

High diversity in older areas. Places that are more diverse in terms of ethnic residential mixing do not necessarily have a great deal of social contact between the groups. However, it seems likely that conversations, mutual assistance, and friendships among neighbors and children of different groups are much more common in such places than in low-diversity places.

Highly diverse areas tend to have housing prices that are moderate—neither extremely low nor extremely high. This means that each of the different groups has reasonably good opportunities to live in those neighborhoods. In the central part of Los Angeles County they appear as a ring that mostly encircles the lowest-cost housing areas east and south of Downtown L.A. Inside the ring are very high proportions of either Latinos or Latinos and Blacks. This is often because many members of these groups cannot afford better housing elsewhere.

Most of the high-diversity ring itself contains somewhat better quality housing. Depending on the area, either Asians or Whites, or both together, may be dominant, but usually some combination of Latinos and Blacks is also present. Thus, the ring represents an ethnic and economic transition zone. Similar

situations occur in the middle of the San Fernando Valley and in northern Orange County, both of which are moderately priced older suburban areas dating from the 1950s and 1960s.

Access to Porter Ranch suburb

Highly diverse newer suburbs. Many of the outermost suburbs are also highly diverse because the low prices of homes built there since about 1970 have attracted people of moderate means from all ethnic groups. This can be seen in Palmdale and Lancaster and in most newer sections of Riverside and San Bernardino Counties.

Some of ethnic diversity in those areas represents families, particularly Black or Latino, who came to these areas through service in the armed forces. Families stationed in the 1980s at either George Air Force Base north of Victorville, Norton A.F.B. in San Bernardino, or March A.F.B. south of Riverside usually lived off the base, and strong social ties with the local population were often made over the years. The high ethnic diversity on and near military installations is clearly the result of early desegregation of the U.S. military soon after World War II and non-discriminatory recruitment practices. Before Census 2000 all these military facilities in Southern California had been either closed or, in the case of March A.F.B., converted to a reservist base. The diversity of earlier military times persists because of marriages with local people and some preferences for retirement in the local area.

The eastern San Gabriel Valley has been attractive to Whites and Asians. When some Latinos or Blacks also reside in the area, the diversity is increased substantially. Homes in upscale Walnut and Diamond Bar were mostly constructed in the 1980s and have been sought after by more affluent families of all ethnic groups. Relationships between groups in the city of Walnut seem to be amicable with much close social mixing of children of different ethnicities in schools.[3] Walnut can be considered a test case of interethnic relationships in an affluent suburb of modern America. The situation in Cerritos has been similar, although that city has become less diverse in recent

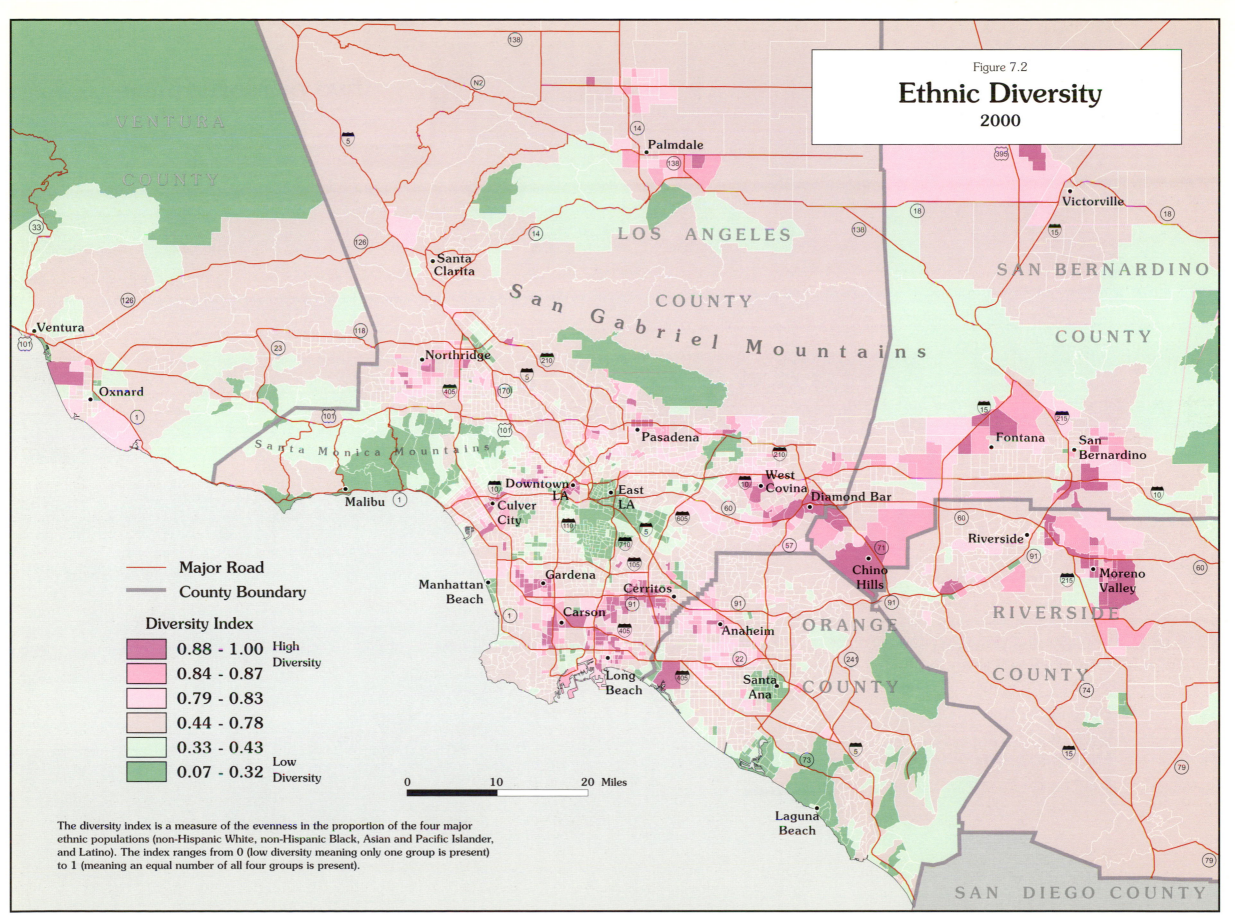

Figure 7.2
Ethnic Diversity
2000

Major Road

County Boundary

Diversity Index

0.88 - 1.00	High Diversity
0.84 - 0.87	
0.79 - 0.83	
0.44 - 0.78	
0.33 - 0.43	
0.07 - 0.32	Low Diversity

0   10   20 Miles

The diversity index is a measure of the evenness in the proportion of the four major ethnic populations (non-Hispanic White, non-Hispanic Black, Asian and Pacific Islander, and Latino). The index ranges from 0 (low diversity meaning only one group is present) to 1 (meaning an equal number of all four groups is present).

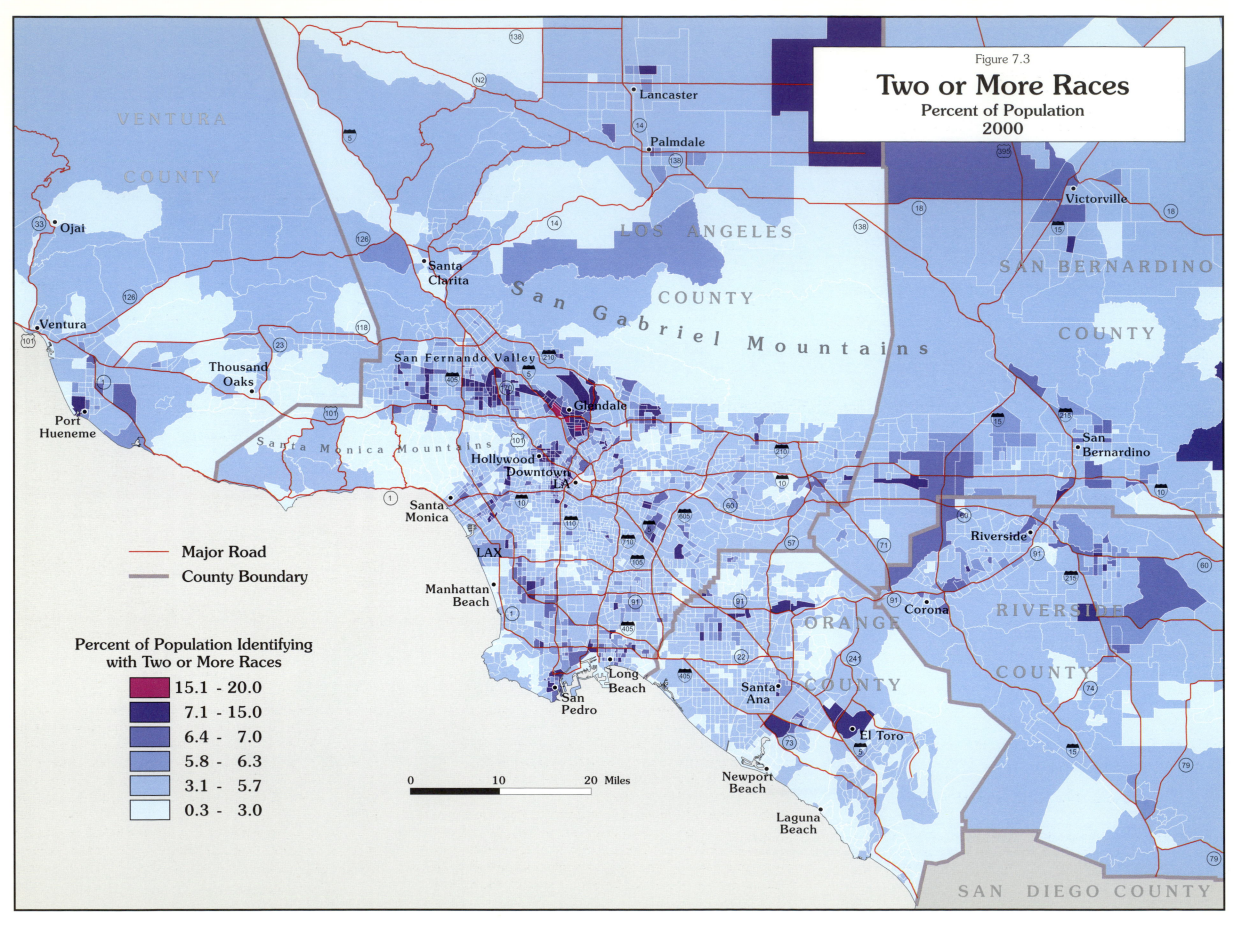

Figure 7.3

Two or More Races

Percent of Population
2000

Major Road

County Boundary

Percent of Population Identifying
with Two or More Races

15.1 - 20.0
7.1 - 15.0
6.4 - 7.0
5.8 - 6.3
3.1 - 5.7
0.3 - 3.0

0   10   20 Miles

years as the homes of Whites, Latinos, and Blacks who moved out have been regularly bought by Asians.

Poor areas of low diversity. Diversity is unusually low in the poorest and richest areas of Southern California. The poorer areas were formerly more diverse, but during the 1980s and 1990s Latino in-movement was unusually strong. Blacks had previously been most numerous in many of these poor areas, but low-income members of other groups were sometimes present also. When Latinos large-ly replaced these other groups, the area became low in diversity.

This process has taken place south and east of L.A.'s central area. Once ethnically diverse Boyle Heights has become highly Latino, as have Bell, Huntington Park and nearby cities such as Maywood and South Gate. The same change has occurred in

Broadway, Downtown L.A.

Santa Ana in Orange County and in the East San Fernando Valley, where the poorest sections of the city of San Fernando and the adjacent Pacoima area of Los Angeles City are now mostly Latino. Older neighborhoods in the central parts of cities like Oxnard, Corona, Riverside and San Bernardino also have low diversity because their low-cost housing has attracted poor Latinos but few others.

Affluent areas of low diversity. At the other extreme are areas in which housing is so expensive that it is affordable to some Whites but few members of the other groups. These areas usually have attractive environmental settings, such as in the mountains, in canyons, or close to popular beach-es. Such high-status areas are in the Santa Monica Mountains and nearby Beverly Hills and along the coast at Malibu and Manhattan Beach and in the coastal communities of Orange County like Laguna Beach.

People of Multiracial Heritage

Because of increasing intermarriage between members of different ethnic groups and the growing number of mixed-race children, this new census category will become more important in the future, particularly in California. In the United States 2.4

percent of the population reported more than one race. However, the mixed-race percentage was 4.7 in both the state of California as a whole and the five-county Southern California area.[4] The only state with a higher percentage of mixed-race people was Hawaii, where 21.4 percent of the residents marked two or more races.

Table 7.1. Largest Mixed-race Populations, 2000: Los Angeles CMSA

Combination	Total	Non-Latino Only
White-Some Other Race	389,701	101,809
White-Asian	98,873	89,083
White-American Indian	62,779	43,404
White-Black	43,589	36,195
Asian-Some Other Race	36,830	23,086
Black-Some Other Race	25,787	9,406
Total Mixed-race	770,483	378,088

Source: U.S. Census Bureau (2002b).

Of the 770,000 people in Southern California who report-ed more than one racial identity, 51 percent identified them-selves as White and Some Other Race (Table 7.1). Other com-binations were much less common. Because many people with mixed-race identities are Latino, we distinguish between Latino and non-Latino mixed-race numbers. For example, 74 percent of the group reporting themselves as both White and Some Other Race were Latino. It is likely that most of these Latinos had a primary identity as Latino and found it difficult to fit themselves clearly into the census race categories.

The value of mapping specific mixed-race combinations is diminished by the small number of people in each mixed-race combination and their widespread distribution. At the same time, the pattern of areal variations in mixed-race percentages is difficult to interpret because so many different group combi-nations are included (Figure 7.3).[5]

The largest areas indicated as multiracial are in the San Fernando Valley and in Glendale. Many people reporting more than one race were undoubtedly Latinos who marked both "White" and "Some Other Race." In addition, because Glendale is home to so many Armenians, it seems likely that the mixed-race concentration in Glendale represents primarily Armenians, who checked "White" and "Some other Race" but wrote in "Armenian" as the other race.

Some other tracts with high proportions of people report-ing two or more races are associated with military installations, where relations between Blacks and Whites have often been closer than in the civilian world. In Ventura County the Port Hueneme Seabee Battalion stands out, as does the Orange

County tract near the El Toro Marine Corps Air Station, which was closed in the late 1990s.

Describing Levels of Residential Separation

At this point we change from maps as indicators of the geography of ethnic distributions to a statistical measure that summarizes how similar or different any two ethnic distribu-tions are.

The index of dissimilarity. This statistic, also called the segregation index, indicates the degree of residential sepa-ration or segregation between any two groups by measuring how much the two distributions differ.[6] The index, referred to as D, provides a convenient summary statement of the extent to which two groups live in different neighborhoods. It is particu-larly useful for comparing levels of spatial separation over time, differences between groups, and differences between places.

"Fancy Shawl" dancer at a powwow

The index ranges from 0 to 1, with 1 representing com-plete segregation—where neither of the two groups occupies any of the same neighborhoods or tracts. A score of 0 indicates that the two groups are distributed in all the same tracts and that their proportions in each tract equal their proportions in the entire metropolitan area. Any specific value of the index can be thought of as the percentage of one group's members that would have to be redistributed in order to create the same dis-tribution as the other group. For example, the D value of .38 for Black-White separation in Orange County in 2000 means that 38 percent of either Blacks or Whites would have to move to different census tracts if the two distributions were to be made equal (Table 7.2).

Table 7.2. Residential Separation, 1980, 1990 and 2000: Counties in Los Angeles CMSA

Blacks, Hispanics, and Asians in Comparison to Whites

Index of Dissimilarity

Black - White	1980	1990	2000
Los Angeles	.81	.73	.67
Orange	.45	.38	.38
Riverside	.54	.47	.47
San Bernardino	.53	.40	.41
Ventura	55	.48	.47
U.S. Average (large metro areas)	78	.72	.68

Latino - White			
Los Angeles	.57	.61	.63
Orange	.42	.50	.55
Riverside	.40	.35	.42
San Bernardino	.37	.36	.43
Ventura	.53	.52	.56
U.S. Average (large metro areas)	.53	.53	.54

Asian and Pacific Islander - White			
Los Angeles	.47	.46	.49
Orange	.27	.33	.40
Riverside	.31	.35	.36
San Bernardino	.26	.32	.37
Ventura	.37	30	.30
U.S. Average (large metro areas)	.41	.42	.43

Sources: Southern California counties in 2000: calculations by the authors. U.S. averages in 1990 and 2000: Houston et al. (2001b). Southern California counties in 1980 and 1990: Clark (1996), 118-121. U.S. averages in 1980: Harrison and Weinberg (1992).

Notes: U.S. large metro averages are based on the 61 metropolitan areas with over one million population in 2000. These contain 65 percent of the population in U.S. metro areas and 52 percent of the total U.S. population. For Southern California counties in 2000, people reporting more than one race were fractionally assigned to the appropriate groups, as explained in chapter 2. Differences between our dissimilarity indexes and those of others who included all mixed-race Whites in the non-White race totals (McConville and Ong 2001; Houston et al. 2001) were insignificant—less than .01.

Place differences in levels of separation. Levels of separation in 2000 between Whites and the other groups were clearly higher in Los Angeles County than in the four surrounding counties. Moreover, separation in Los Angeles was higher than most other places in California. Black-White separation and Latino-White separation were higher in Los Angeles County than in any other metropolitan area in the state.[7] Asian-White separation in California was highest in Los Angeles, San Francisco, and Sacramento, which were essentially equal in their indexes of dissimilarity.

These observations are consistent with much research comparing metropolitan areas nationally.[8] Separation is typically higher in larger metropolitan areas than in smaller ones and higher where the ethnic group being compared to Whites comprises a greater proportion of the total population. In addition, separation levels tend to be lower where there are higher proportions of newer housing, most commonly in rapidly expanding suburbs.

In Southern California the greater separation in Los Angeles County is understandable when one considers that the ethnic and social class character of many of its neighborhoods were established decades ago, when housing discrimination was legal and ubiquitous. In contrast, the four outlying counties contain greater proportions of newer suburban housing, into which Blacks, Hispanics, and Asians have been able to move during recent decades. Within those four outlying counties, separation has been somewhat less in neighborhoods where levels of income and educational attainment are higher.[9]

With respect to Black-White separation, Orange, Riverside, and San Bernardino Counties have clearly lower levels of Black-White separation than the U.S. average, with separation particularly low in Orange County. Ventura County, with a population of only 753,000, is less segregated than the average middle-size metropolitan area, for which the index of dissimilarity was .57. These lower levels of Black-White separation are related to the newer suburban developments and the historically smaller Black populations in outlying counties.

Latino-White separation in Los Angeles County is clearly greater than the average found in large metropolitan areas.[10] Of the fifty largest metropolitan areas in the United States, only New York and Newark, NJ, have a higher level of separation. And of 331 U.S. metropolitan areas, the only places apart from New York and Newark with higher Latino-White separation than Los Angeles County are four smaller metropolitan areas in the Northeast. Separation levels in Orange and Ventura Counties are similar to the national average, and Riverside and San Bernardino Counties are less segregated than average.

Nationally, Asian-White separation was slightly higher in Los Angeles County than in most other large metropolitan areas.[11] Whites and Asians were similarly separated in New York (D = .50) as in Los Angeles; but Atlanta, Boston, Chicago, Detroit, and Houston also had index values of .44 or higher. In the four outlying counties Asian-White separation was lower than the average for large metropolitan areas. The relatively higher level of separation in Orange County can be explained by its unusually large Vietnamese enclave, Little Saigon.

General separation trends. Black-White separation has dropped since 1980, whereas Latino-White separation has increased. With the exception of Ventura County, Asians and Whites also became slightly more separated. Because Whites generally lived in different tracts from the other groups, one factor that tends to reduce measured separation in Los Angeles County is simply the large decline in numbers of Whites.

Chino Hills

Trends in Black-White separation. In 1960 Chicago was the most racially segregated metropolitan area in the United States, and Los Angeles County and Milwaukee were tied as the second most segregated.[12] The 1960 index of dissimilarity for Los Angeles was .90. Since then, segregation in Los Angeles County has declined more rapidly than in most other large metro areas so that Black-White separation now equals the average of all large metropolitan areas.

The reduction in Black-White separation in Los Angeles County is striking when compared to the current higher levels for well known Eastern and Midwestern metro areas. Whereas Los Angeles County's segregation index value in 2000 was .67, that for Detroit was .85 and Chicago, Gary, Milwaukee, New York, and Newark all had values of .80 or higher.

A major factor in the declining Black-White separation of the four outlying counties has been Black settlement in the newer suburban developments of those counties. In many such places home prices are much lower than in Los Angeles County, and nowadays discrimination against Black potential renters or homeowners is much less than it was in the 1970s and earlier.

The above trends are fairly typical of metropolitan areas across the country. Nationally, Black-White separation during the 1990s continued the decline that began in 1970 and is now lower than at any time since 1920.[13] The largest declines during the 1990s occurred in more rapidly growing areas with smaller Black populations. Black-White separation also decreased more rapidly in metropolitan areas that have been receiving the most immigrants, that is, where Hispanic and Asian proportions have been growing.[14]

Trends in Latino-White separation. Although Blacks have traditionally been the group most segregated from Whites, in some areas Latinos have become more segregated than Blacks. In 2000 Latinos and Whites in both Orange and Ventura Counties were more segregated than Blacks and Whites. In Los Angeles County, Black-White separation was only slightly higher than Latino-White separation.

Latino-White separation has risen somewhat in all five counties, with the largest increase in Orange County. In Los Angeles County Latino-White separation has increased slowly since 1960, when the index of dissimilarity was .55.[15]

The increase in separation in Southern California mirrors national trends in areas with higher percentages of Latinos. In the 1990s Latino separation increased slightly in those metropolitan areas that were over 10 percent Hispanic.[16]

Riverside County's trend of separation was unusual because it was lower in 1990 than in either 1980 or 2000. The increased Latino-White separation as of 2000 may have been related to the great expansion of new home construction during the 1990s. It is possible that during the 1980s Latinos were moving into many mostly White neighborhoods, but in the 1990s many Whites left these areas. Homes in a greater range of prices may have become available so that Whites with their higher average income levels were able to buy more easily the more expensive homes in the county.

Trends in Asian-White separation. The measured increase in separation in Los Angeles County reflects the increased Asian settlement in enclaves. The increase was greater in Orange, Riverside, and San Bernardino Counties and is presumably related to the growing Asian populations settling there. The decline in Ventura County may reflect the earlier high level of separation of Japanese and Filipinos in enclaves in the Oxnard area compared to the greater suburban dispersal of more recent Asian arrivals to the county.

Explaining the Persistence of Residential Separation

The patterns and trends presented so far have been discussed mostly in terms of demographic characteristics—the size of metropolitan populations and their ethnic proportions—as well as proportions of new housing in different metro areas.

These describe but do not explain the widespread persistence of moderately high levels of residential separation.

To better understand forces behind changes in levels of separation, certain influences must be examined. We discuss first the attitudes and perceptions of members of the different ethnic groups toward their own and other groups, which some people believe is the most important explanation of continued separation. Then we look at ethnic group differences in financial resources and ethnic discrimination in the housing market.

Ethnic attitudes. Many people wish to live among people of their own ethnic group. This means not that they prefer ethnically homogeneous neighborhoods but that they feel more comfortable where members of their group are commonly found. Such an attitude is widespread and somewhat more frequently found among recent immigrants, who often depend on nearby friends, relatives, and ethnic institutions to help them in their adjustment.[17] To the extent that people choose where to live on the basis of an own-group preference, the index of dissimilarity will show higher values.

Two major studies of Los Angeles County residents, one in 1987 and the other in the early 1990s, investigated group attitudes carefully and in much greater detail than can be reported here.[18] All ethnic groups reported a preference for their own group as neighbors, and some degree of ethnic cohesiveness undoubtedly prompts some people to locate where other members of their group live. Groups differed, however, in the strength of their prejudices toward other groups and what would be an acceptable neighborhood ethnic composition.

In the 1987 survey, Whites had the strongest preferences for neighborhoods in which Whites comprised a high proportion of residents, and both Whites and Asians avoided neighborhoods where Blacks constitute more than 10 percent of the residents. For neighbors outside one's own group, Whites were consistently the most preferred and Blacks the least preferred. Whites evaluated Blacks and Latinos in the neighborhood similarly, and 60 percent of Whites wanted neighborhoods that were at least 80 percent White. All such preferences suggest the possibility of a tipping point, a percentage value at which Whites or others will tend to move out of their neighborhood. However, no such point has been identified, and it would clearly differ depending on the groups involved.

The early 1990s research found that homeowners, foreign-born Latinos, and foreign-born Asians preferred fewer Black neighbors than did Whites, renters, and U.S.-born Latinos and Asians. Both Blacks and U.S.-born Asians accepted larger proportions of Latinos in their neighborhood than did Whites. Latinos wanted a high proportion of their group in the neighborhood but were willing to move into a mixed neighborhood if the other residents were White. Because such attitudes continue to be important in people's choice of neighborhoods, the persistence of residential separation should not be surprising.

Financial resources. Ethnic differences in income and wealth are also factors in separation. Because White and Asian households have higher incomes than the average Black or Latino household, these greater financial resources make it possible for Whites and Asians to rent or buy in somewhat higher-priced neighborhoods (Table 7.3).

Table 7.3. Median Household Income, Major Ethnic Groups, 1990: Los Angeles CMSA

Ethnic Group	Income
Non-Hispanic White	$41,544
Latino	$26,625
Black	$28,891
Asian and Pacific Islander	$40,724

Source: U.S. Census Bureau 1993b.

Moreover, increased Latino-White separation since 1980 may be partly explained by the fact that the income gap between the two groups has been growing wider over the last few decades.[19] This means that, on the average, fewer Latinos can afford to live in the same neighborhoods as Whites than was the case forty years ago. In other words, housing markets for the two groups may have become increasingly separate for economic reasons alone.

The fact that Asians and Whites are moderately separated even though their average incomes are similar suggests the importance of non-economic factors in maintaining separation.

Federal policies and discrimination. Since World War II policies of the federal government regarding taxation, transportation, and homeownership have tended to promote homeownership in new suburbs that were nearly all White rather than in older areas where minorities usually lived.[20] To the extent that Whites benefited disproportionately from those policies, central cities had higher proportions of minorities and suburbs had higher proportions of Whites than they otherwise would have had.

As for discrimination in the sale or rental of housing in the suburbs, it has diminished a great deal since the 1960s.[21] However, there is evidence that housing discrimination continues nationally and in Los Angeles despite being illegal.[22]

Discrimination affecting home sales seems to occur most commonly when potential buyers are hoping for approval of their mortgage application by the lender. Approval of home loans, including those federally insured through the FHA, is less likely for Latinos and Blacks than for Whites, both in Southern California suburban counties and in Los Angeles County.[23] In addition, Blacks and Latinos are more likely than Whites to seek mortgages from subprime lenders, who charge higher interest rates and occasionally excessive fees.[24]

Discrimination in apartment rentals is no longer just a matter of White landlords refusing to rent to Black, Latino, or Asian tenants. Members of many ethnic groups, frequently immigrants, own or manage apartment buildings, and their own ethnic biases clearly affect their treatment of prospective tenants.[25] In many cases they try to replace the often ethnically diverse tenants with members of their own ethnic group, probably for better control.[26] Although such practices presumably lead toward the greater ethnic homogeneity of residents of individual apartment buildings, at the census-tract level they may have little impact on residential separation.

In addition, some realtors may subtly steer their clients to neighborhoods where the client's own ethnic group is better represented. Such a practice acts to increase ethnic separation.

Explaining Small Recent Shifts in Separation Levels

The prior section explained the factors behind generally moderate or high levels of ethnic residential separation in Southern California and the United States. However, small changes in the levels of separation observed since 1980 can be best understood as shifts in the balance between those factors promoting and other factors diminishing separation. The tension between these opposing influences produces a net effect, which is measurable each decade.

Factors favoring ethnic residential mixing. Cultural change, assimilation, and higher income levels tend to increase ethnic dispersal from enclaves and reduce residential separation. Also, attitudes toward other groups can become more favorable over time, leading toward less discomfort with more mixed neighborhoods. This may have occurred to some extent since the late 1980s and early 1990s, when the Los Angeles data on ethnic and neighborhood attitudes reported earlier in this chapter was collected.[27]

Other factors tending to diminish residential separation are the cultural assimilation of immigrants and their children, the desire to escape the problems of poor areas, and greater income that may make the move possible. We expect that the desire to move out of a low-income ethnic enclave is prompted more by economic considerations than by ethnic attitudes.

Rates of crime are probably higher in poor enclaves, and schools there are often of lower quality.

Many Blacks, in particular, have wanted to leave Black enclaves—the old ghetto areas into which they had been forced earlier by White society. Civil rights laws, improved education and earnings, and shifts in social attitudes have made departure much more possible in recent decades.

Factors favoring ethnic separation. New immigrants frequently locate near friends and relatives who can help them adjust, leading frequently to the growth of ethnic enclaves. Thus, if the number of new immigrants is very large, as it has been in Southern California, this tendency toward ethnic neighborhood concentration may more than balance the countervailing tendency of the more assimilated and successful members of the group to move out of those enclaves.

Also, some people with the economic means to move out of enclaves may choose not to do so because they are more comfortable in neighborhoods where their group is well represented. In some cases, this may reflect concerns about their treatment by members of other groups.

The net balance. For Blacks in Southern California, declining separation seems clearly related to rising social and economic opportunities in recent decades, exemplified by growing numbers of middle-class Blacks.

For Latinos and Asians the trends are more problematic. The small increase in Asian-White segregation during the 1990s is consistent with the growing proportion of most Asian groups living in enclaves (Table 6.2). Many Asians leave ethnic enclaves, but they are more than balanced by others who move in. As explained near the end of chapter 6, most of the Asian enclaves are not in poor areas. It appears, then, that the increased residential separation of Asians reflects a widespread desire to live within a clearly Asian neighborhood.

In the case of Latinos, increased separation from Whites is best explained by the large number of poor immigrants who arrived during the 1990s and the growing White-Mexican income gap. This gap is closely related to a growing spread during the 1990s between the incomes of the poor and the more affluent in California.[28] These factors appear to have outweighed slightly the strong countervailing tendencies of dispersal associated with cultural and economic assimilation.

Notes

1. For a detailed analysis of the changing levels of ethnic diversity in different Southern California cities (rather than neighborhoods), see Myers and Park (2001).

2. The method of calculation and properties of the entropy index compared to other statistics are explained in White (1986).

3. O'Connor (1999).

4. U.S. Census Bureau (2001f).

5. In addition to the patterns on the map, tract 9200.27 (east of Bouquet Canyon, north of Santa Clarita) was also 20 percent multiracial. However, the tract contained only 3 mixed-race people out of a total population of 15. Because it would be distracting and highly misleading to show this large area in the intense high-percentage category, the tract appears on this map in the lowest percent category.

6. The calculation and properties of the dissimilarity index compared to other statistics are explained in White (1986) and in Massey and Denton (1988).

7. Houston et al. (2001a).

8. Comparisons between the Los Angeles area and the United States rely on Houston et al. (2001b). Other useful national analyses are Frey and Farley (1996), McConville and Ong (2001), and Logan (2001a).

9. Clark and Ware (1997).

10. Logan (2001a); Houston et al. (2001b).

11. Houston et al. (2001b).

12. Allen and Turner (1996a), 19.

13. Glaeser and Vigdor (2001).

14. Frey and Farley (1996).

15. Moore and Mittlebach (1966).

16. Logan (2001a).

17. Allen and Turner (1996b); Massey (1985).

18. One study by Clark (1992) used a 1987 telephone survey of over 2,600 households. The other by Charles (2000a, b) was based on interviews in 1993-1994 with a sample of over 4,000 residents. We suspect that attitudes toward other groups may have improved somewhat since the early 1990s, a period of severe recession in Los Angeles with ethnic tensions resulting from the 1992 riots.

19. Allen and Turner (1997), 172-179.

20. Drier, Mollenkopf, and Swanstrom (2001), 92-132.

21. De Graaf (2001), 422-423.

22. Reibel (2000); Dymski and Veitch (1994); Yinger (1995).

23. Aldana and Dymski (2001); Wedner (2001). Research on possible discrimination by mortgage lenders often makes use of federal Home Mortgage Disclosure Act data, which does not include information on the credit history and debts of applicants. Nevertheless, research by Reibel in Los Angeles County as of 1990 found strong indications of discrimination against Black applicants. Moreover, "there is evidence that Black and Hispanic applicants are treated more favorably when they apply for mortgages in predominantly Black areas, and Hispanic applicants also receive more favorable treatment when they apply in predominantly Hispanic areas" (Reibel 2000, 58). Such discrimination tends to reinforce ethnic residential separation.

24. Stein and Libby (2001).

25. Rohrlich (1999).

26. Fox (2001).

27. Clark (1992); Charles (2000a, b).

28. Reed (1999).

8. Conclusion

The ethnic transformation of Southern California that began in the late 1960s continues to this day. Just as the faces of Southern Californians have been changing, so have the places. The tendency of many members of all ethnic groups to live in some places much more than others demonstrates the role of ethnicity in people's residential decisions. Ethnic spatial patterning is a significant dimension of society.

Because of our geographical emphasis on places, the details of our maps and interpretations are at least as important as our more general findings. Nevertheless, *Changing Faces, Changing Places* does present results for the region as a whole, which we develop in the next sections.

Suburbanization of all Ethnic Groups

All ethnic groups have been deconcentrating residentially. Whites, having abandoned central city locations decades ago, tended to leave older suburban neighborhoods during the 1990s. Some settled in newer and more affluent suburbs, and others moved out of Southern California entirely. Because the numbers of Whites in Southern California declined by 10 percent during the 1990s, much housing became available for members of other groups.

The large and fast-growing Latino population represented the greatest component of change in the 1990s. Latinos typically occupy less costly housing in older neighborhoods and have been moving into both older White suburbs and formerly Black areas of central cities. Blacks, at a much later stage of suburbanization, have been leaving older, more central neighborhoods during the last two or three decades. Many Asians, with their above-average incomes, dispersed into more expensive and mostly White suburbs. Others, particularly immigrants, settled in Asian enclaves. Asian increases were most pronounced in upscale suburban Asian concentrations, some of which have become attractive to several Asian groups, resulting in multiethnic Asian or pan-Asian enclaves. Although our maps have

tended to emphasize the various ethnic concentrations, it is important to realize that many business, cultural, and political leaders of all ethnic groups live outside such concentrations or on their fringes.

The maps demonstrate that many thousands of households in all groups have moved closer to the metropolitan fringe. For this reason, ethnic diversity tends to be high in these outer suburban areas. Diversity is also high in some older suburbs. Diversity is lowest at both economic extremes—in the strongly Latino areas, which are poor and from which other groups have left, and strongly White areas, where houses are extremely expensive.

Ethnic Residential Separation and Enclaves

The tendency of Whites to live in more affluent, strongly White enclaves diminished during the 1990s. Other groups are entering those neighborhoods to some extent. Research has shown that Whites in Southern California are less residentially isolated than Whites in the comparable metropolitan areas (CMSAs) of New York or Chicago.[1] As of 2000, only 22 percent of Whites in Los Angeles lived in census tracts that were over 80 percent White, whereas in Chicago and New York just over 60 percent of Whites lived in tracts that were over 80 percent White.

Black-White separation. This is still high in Los Angeles County but has been diminishing steadily for more than three decades. Moreover, Blacks and Whites are much less separated residentially in Southern California than in other large metropolitan areas in the East and Midwest. New York, Chicago, Detroit, and Milwaukee are the most highly segregated large metropolitan areas in the United States. When this relatively lower level of Black-White separation in Los Angeles County is combined with the much lower levels in the four outlying suburban counties, it is clear that in Southern California

Blacks are much less separated residentially from Whites than in the other very large metropolitan areas.

Nevertheless, some people believe that housing discrimination in Southern California remains as powerful as it was thirty or forty years ago and that Black-White segregation continues at a very high level in Los Angeles. We suspect some such opinions are based on the assumption that racist practices continue at the same level indefinitely and on generalization from Eastern and Midwestern metropolitan areas, with which some scholars may be more familiar. In contrast, our perception—as residents of Southern California—is that such assessments for Southern California are twenty years behind the times. Race, racism, and race-based discrimination are still significant here, but they have diminished substantially.

Latino-White separation. On the average Latinos and Whites in Southern California are about as separated residentially as are Blacks and Whites, but the five counties differ as to the most highly separated group. Some Americans may have assumed that Blacks and Whites would remain more separated than any other groups, but in 2000 Latinos were the group most residentially separated from Whites in Orange, San Bernardino, and Ventura Counties.

In Los Angeles County the level of Latino-White residential separation is among the highest in the United States. Separation is slightly higher in the comparable metropolitan area of New York and slightly lower in Chicago, but all other large metropolitan areas have lower indexes of separation.

White-Latino separation is unusually high in Los Angeles County and moderately high in Orange and Ventura Counties because of two key factors: the very large numbers of Latino immigrants who arrived recently and the large and growing Latino-White income gap. Most immigrants from Mexico have settled in neighborhoods with other Mexicans, where housing costs are lower and where they are more comfortable. Also, most arrive here lacking much money, good English-language skills, or the advanced education that could lead to better jobs and higher incomes, which could prompt relocation outside strongly Mexican neighborhoods.

In contrast, Latino-White separation is less in Riverside and San Bernardino Counties because Latinos in these counties tend not to be immigrants themselves. Rather, they are more likely to be the assimilated and economically successful children and grandchildren of earlier immigrants.

Asian-White separation. In Los Angeles County Asians are as separated residentially from Whites as they are in San Francisco, New York, and Houston. These four places have the highest levels of White-Asian separation of any large metropolitan areas in the United States.

Because the average income level of Asians approximates that of Whites, their residential separation from Whites cannot be explained by insufficient economic resources. The slightly increased separation from Whites during the 1990s and the growth of Asian enclaves are due primarily to a preference on the part of Asian immigrants for living near other members of their nationality.

Explaining metropolitan differences in ethnic separation. The relative levels of separation measured in different metropolitan areas do not fit any simple explanation. Nevertheless, our findings for different Southern California counties, in combination with other research across the United States, suggest that ethnic populations in smaller and more rapidly growing metropolitan areas in the Western states tend to be less separated residentially. Conversely, large numbers and high proportions of recent immigrants appear to increase group residential separation. Because differences among metropolitan areas in racial attitudes and ethnic group income disparities are probably small, we expect that relative levels of ethnic residential separation in different places can be best explained by basic demographic factors—the numbers and proportions of groups and the relative timing of their arrival.

The Meaning of Ethnic Enclaves Today

Strength and growth of enclaves. The maps and enclave percentage tables in this book make it clear that ethnic areal concentrations or enclaves remain strong in Southern California. Half of all Latinos and more than half of all Whites live in census tracts in which 60 percent of the residents are members of those respective groups. Among the smaller groups, the percentage living in enclaves ranges from 30 to 60 percent. Enclave settlement has been growing in importance for Latinos, Mexicans, and most Asian groups but diminishing for Whites, Filipinos, Central Americans, and Blacks.

Some scholars have imagined that the ease of transportation and communication within a modern metropolis should make enclave settlement of little importance for upper- and middle-class immigrants.[2] According to this view, immigrants are able to stay well connected with their ethnic communities without having to live in a residential concentration. Although this situation applies to the many immigrants and children of immigrants who choose to live outside ethnic enclaves, the evidence of Asian enclave growth presented in this book demonstrates that enclaves remain important for large numbers of people.[3]

Explaining contemporary enclaves. Because of the heritage of racism and enforced racial segregation in this country, some Americans may assume that present-day ethnic concentrations or enclaves represent a malignancy—a pernicious vestige of the past that should no longer exist. However, over the last few decades, the factors explaining enclave formation and persistence in Southern California have changed. Although ethnic enclaves in poor neighborhoods do reflect the economic limitations of their residents, the fact that they are ethnic concentrations and not just poverty concentrations suggests that people's decisions as to residential location are based on both economic constraints and shared ethnic identity. Moreover, the existence and growth of Asian enclaves in high-status suburbs demonstrates the importance of ethnic concentrations for many immigrants who have sufficient resources to live elsewhere.

Mobility out of poor enclaves. Members of ethnic groups do make economic progress, enabling them to move out of older, central city neighborhoods into better areas. Their places in those enclaves then become occupied by new poor people, usually recent immigrants. Because the census reports the characteristics of neighborhoods every ten years as opposed to tracking the original residents and their changing fortunes, comparing the characteristics of places like poor enclaves over time easily misses the progress that individuals and families make.[4]

This progress is illustrated by the upward and outward movement of Mexicans from Boyle Heights and East Los Angeles toward newer suburbs farther east, as well as the residential shift of members of all ethnic groups out of Los Angeles City.[5] Homeownership gives 40 percent of Black households and 33 percent of Latino households in South Central Los Angeles the means to leave that area by selling their homes if they wish. Also, Maya Indians from Guatemala have found ways to move out of their poor enclave in Pico-Union, although many at the time of their arrival had lacked language skills in both English and Spanish.

Because of the turnover and potential turnover of population in poorer enclaves and the existence of higher-status Asian enclaves, contemporary enclaves in Southern California should be thought of as essentially voluntary or self-selected rather than imposed as a result of discrimination or prejudice. This is the reason why urban scholars Peter Marcuse and Ronald van Kempen assess modern-day enclaves as follows. "In principle, there is no reason why public policy should interfere with enclave formation, so long as it is truly voluntary, that is, that anyone resident in an enclave has the realistic possibility of moving out."[6]

Reduced assimilation in large enclaves? Although we have emphasized the choices of individuals in explaining contemporary enclaves, enclaves may have another meaning for the larger Southern California society. In this different perspective, the presence and growth of enclaves may retard the development of English-language skills, education, and general cultural and economic assimilation that should be available for newcomers. Moreover, as some ethnic groups are found in increasing proportions in enclaves, ethnic group isolation and divisions between groups can be expected to increase. Although factors other than enclave residence are probably more important influences on the adaptation of immigrants, we do caution that enclave growth probably tends to heighten social and cultural divisions between ethnic groups.[7]

The high and growing percentage of Latinos in enclaves is particularly noteworthy. Such an ethnic geographical divide would appear to reinforce the growing White-Mexican gap in median income. Because Asian enclaves are more mixed ethnically and average Asian incomes are much higher, the potential for isolation of Asians seems much less than for Latinos, particularly Mexicans.

Improvements with Local Residential Mobility

Many of the patterns of ethnic change that are mapped in this book were interpreted as residential shifts into higher-status neighborhoods. For Whites, Blacks, and Asians, the most common change during the 1990s involved movement into newer, higher-priced suburbs. Although the pattern of Latino increase was strongest in and near enclaves (barrios) in central cities and older suburbs, Latinos also settled in newer and somewhat more expensive suburbs. From the point of view of individual households, the net result of these changes seems positive in that it reflects an improved economic or housing status. All major ethnic groups participated strongly in these shifts into newer suburbs. This suggests that past constraints on inequality of opportunity have been substantially weakened, at least among a major portion of each group's population.

Table 8.1. Ratings of Present Residence Compared to Previous Residence among Recent Movers, 1999: Los Angeles County

	Percent of Householders of Each Ethnic Group		
	White/ Asian	Black	Latino
Better home	51.6	55.4	61.0
Worse home	21.7	21.3	13.4
Better neighborhood	38.5	57.7	47.4
Worse neighborhood	20.4	18.1	13.7

Source: U.S. Census Bureau 2001a.

Notes: This table is based on the 18 percent of householders who moved within the previous year. Percentages for each group for either home or neighborhood do not sum to 100 because the columns do not include those that rate their present home and neighborhood about the same as their previous one. The Whites/Asians category also includes Non-Hispanic American Indians. For the complete survey in Los Angeles County, 2851 householders were interviewed.

Table 8.2. Ratings of Present Residence Compared to Previous Residence among Recent Movers, 1994: Riverside and San Bernardino Counties

	Percent of Householders of Each Ethnic Group		
	White/ Asian	Black	Latino
Better home	55.9	61.9	64.3
Worse home	17.0	20.1	14.9
Better neighborhood	51.6	48.0	56.2
Worse neighborhood	18.4	19.0	13.3

Source: U.S. Census Bureau (1996).

Notes: This table is based on the 22 percent of householders who moved within the previous year. For the complete survey in Riverside and San Bernardino Counties, 4,250 householders were interviewed. Also see notes for Table 8.1.

Confirmation of improvement. The fact that most people appear to have moved into better neighborhoods is also evident from the American Housing Surveys taken in 1994 and 1999 (Tables 8.1 and 8.2).

In all three ethnic categories in the tables, more than half of recent movers believed they had moved into better homes. Moreover, movers were two to four times more likely to say that they were in a better neighborhood. Other tables in the original sources make it clear that assessments of improvement were clearly higher among homeowners than among renters.

Differences in evaluation of their moves by householders of different groups and in different counties were not large. The fact that Latinos were most likely to believe their latest move resulted in both a better home and a better neighborhood demonstrates satisfaction with their progress during the 1990s.

Thus, evidence from *Changing Faces, Changing Places* and independent surveys are in agreement that residential mobility has, on the average, led to improved status and satisfaction for Southern Californians, regardless of their ethnic group.

Final Comments

Several of our findings present a positive picture of trends in the 1990s. Increased settlements of all groups in outer suburbs and better neighborhoods, increased homeownership among Blacks and Latinos, and reduced residential separation of Whites, Blacks, and Central Americans are all encouraging. So is the lower level of White isolation and Black-White separation in Southern California compared to New York or Chicago. An important development in urban ethnic geography is that essentially voluntary processes maintain and expand modern ethnic enclaves, particularly those of Asians.

We recognize, however, that the ethnic transformation of Southern California and people's adjustment to a changing economy have not been as smooth as portrayed in our maps and tables. There have been interethnic tensions and resentments related to cultural differences and competition for jobs, housing, and political power. A great many people struggle to survive economically, particularly with the high cost of housing. Learning English is difficult for many people, and often schools are not given the resources to provide the education that children need.

Nevertheless, the arrival of immigrants has infused Southern California with tremendous dynamism, economically and culturally. In some aspects of life, particularly in food, music, and entertainment, there has been much mixing of talent, ideas, and traditions. Many people have found that getting to know individuals in other groups is exhilarating and rewarding. The flows of money and people back and forth between Southern California and about a hundred countries make our region one of the world's centers of both international trade and ethnic diversity.

Although these important and related facets of Southern California are not covered in this book, we hope that *Changing Faces, Changing Places* provides at least a better understanding of the ethnic geographical dimension of life in this region. Moreover, our findings may provide clues as to more general patterns and processes that are currently reshaping American metropolitan areas.

Notes

1. Poulsen et al. (2002).

2. Zelinsky and Lee (1998).

3. Also, *The Ethnic Quilt* contains maps of Asian Indians, Thais, Armenians, Iranians, and Israelis that show middle-class and affluent ethnic enclaves as of 1990. The existence of suburban enclaves, in particular, may not be widely recognized by scholars because theory does not predict them and because many scholars have not mapped ethnic patterns in sufficient detail to discover them. In addition, enclaves may be present only where the ethnic group is large in size. In much smaller metropolitan areas, immigrants might prefer to live in an enclave but local ethnic populations are too small to create one.

4. Myers (1999a) has observed that scholars and politicians often tend to underestimate the mobility of people in and out of poorer neighborhoods because they tend to focus on the changing characteristics of places rather than people.

5. The departure of Mexicans from poorer barrios was shown by Clark and Muller (1988) and Navarro and Acuña (1990). Residential shifts from Los Angeles City to other, more suburban places in Los Angeles County were demonstrated by Myers (1999b), 142-144.

6. Marcuse and van Kempen, eds. (2000), 274.

7. We recognize that the same point could have been made about the divisive effects of White enclaves and White isolation over most decades of the twentieth century.

References

(Note: References to the *Los Angeles Times* are to the San Fernando Valley edition of the *Times*.)

Aldana, C. and G. Dymski. 2001. Federal Housing Policies and Access to Housing in Southern California. Unpublished paper, Department of Economics, UC Riverside.

Allen, J. P. 2002. The Tortilla-Mercedes Divide in Los Angeles. *Political Geography* 21(5): 701-709.

Allen, J. P. and E. Turner. 1996a. Ethnic Diversity and Segregation in the New Los Angeles. In *EthniCity: Geographic Perspectives on Ethnic Change in Modern Cities*, C. C. Roseman, H. D. Laux, and G. Thieme, eds.: 1-29. Lanham, MD: Rowman & Littlefield.

Allen, J. P. and E. Turner. 1996b. Spatial Patterns of Immigrant Assimilation. *The Professional Geographer* 48 (2): 140-155.

Allen, J. P. and E. Turner. 1997. *The Ethnic Quilt: Population Diversity in Southern California*. Northridge, CA: The Center for Geographical Studies, California State University, Northridge.

Allen, J. P. and E. Turner. 2001. Bridging 1990 and 2000 Census Race Data: Fractional Assignment of Multiracial Populations. *Population Research and Policy Review* 20 (6): 513-533.

Alvarez, F. 1995. A Hard Life for Mixtec Laborers. *Los Angeles Times*. July 27: B13.

Bahr, D. 1993. *From Mission to Metropolis: Cupeño Indian Women in Los Angeles*. Norman: University of Oklahoma Press.

Bloom, V. 1959. Oxnard, A Social History of the Early Years. *Ventura County Historical Society Quarterly* 4 (2): 13-20.

Bonvillain, N. 2001. Native Nations of California. In *Native Nations: Culture and Histories of Native North America*, 392-417. Upper Saddle River, NJ: Prentice Hall.

California Department of Finance. 2001. Race/Ethnic Population Estimates: Components of Change for California Counties, April 1990 to July 1999. Demographic Research Unit. http://www.dof.ca.gov

Charles, C. Z. 2000a. Neighborhood Racial-Composition Preferences: Evidence from a Multiethnic Metropolis. *Social Problems* 47 (3): 379-407.

Charles, C. Z. 2000b. Residential Segregation in Los Angeles. In *Prismatic Metropolis: Inequality in Los Angeles*, L. D. Bobo, M. L. Oliver, J. H. Johnson, Jr., and A. Valenzuela, Jr., eds: 167-219. New York: Russell Sage Foundation.

Charles, C. Z. 2001. Processes of Racial Residential Segregation. In *Urban Inequality: Evidence from Four Cities*, A. O'Connor, C. Tilly, and L. D. Bobo, eds.: 217-271. New York: Russell Sage Foundation.

Clark, W. A. V. 1992. Residential Preferences and Residential Choices in a Multi-Ethnic Context. *Demography* 29 (3): 451-466.

Clark, W. A. V. 1996. Residential Patterns: Avoidance, Assimilation, and Succession. In *Ethnic Los Angeles*, R. Waldinger and M. Bozorgmehr, eds: 109-138. New York: Russell Sage Foundation.

Clark, W. A. V. 2000. Monocentric to Policentric: New Urban Forms and Old Paradigms. In *A Companion to the City*, G. Bridge and S. Watson, eds.: 141-154. Oxford, UK, and Malden, MA: Blackwell Publishers.

Clark, W. A. V. 2001. Immigration and the Hispanic Middle Class. Washington, DC: Center for Immigration Studies. http://www.cis.org/articles/2001/hispanicmc/toc.html

Clark, W. A. V. and M. Mueller. 1988. Hispanic Relocation and Spatial Assimilation: A Case Study. *Social Science Quarterly* 69 (2): 468-75.

Clark, W. A. V. and J. Ware. 1997. Trends in Residential Integration by Socioeconomic Status in Southern California. *Urban Affairs Review* 32 (6): 825-843.

Cleeland, N. 1998. Irvine Grows as a Chinese Gateway: Schools, High-Tech Jobs are Magnets Creating a Demographic Shift. *Los Angeles Times*. December 7.

Craine, J. W. 2000. Patterns of Housing Price Change in Los Angeles County, 1988-1999. Unpub. M.A. thesis, Department of Geography, California State University, Northridge.

Dagodag, W. T. 1967. A Social Geography of La Colonia: A Mexican-American Settlement in the City of Oxnard, California. Unpub. M.A. thesis, Department of Geography, San Fernando Valley State College (California State University, Northridge).

De Graaf, L. B. 2001. African American Suburbanization in California, 1960 through 1990. In *Seeking El Dorado: African Americans in California*, L. B. De Graaf, K. Mulroy, and Q. Taylor, eds.: 405-449. Los Angeles and Seattle: Autry Museum of Western Heritage and University of Washington Press.

Drier, P., J. Mollenkopf, and T. Swanstrom. 2001. *Place Matters: Metropolitics for the Twenty-first Century*. Lawrence, KS: University of Kansas Press.

Dymski, G. A. and J. M. Veitch. 1994. Taking It to the Bank: Race, Credit, and Income in Los Angeles. In *Residential Apartheid: The American Legacy*, R. D. Bullard, J. E. Grigsby III, and C. Lee, eds.: 150-179. Los Angeles: Center for Afro-American Studies, UCLA.

Engh, M. E. 2000. At Home in the Heteropolis: Understanding Postmodern L.A. *American Historical Review* 105 (5): 1676-1682. http://www.historycooperative.org/journals/ahr/105.5/ah001676.html

Fields, R. 2001. Puzzling Drop in Latino Groups. *Los Angeles Times*. August 10: B1, 11.

Fong, T. P. 2001. A New and Dynamic Community: The Case of Monterey Park, California. In *Asian and Latino Immigrants in a Restructuring Economy: The Metamorphosis of Southern California*, M. López-Garza and D. Diaz, eds.: 313-331. Stanford: Stanford University Press.

Fox, S. 2001. Mi Case No Es Su Casa. *Los Angeles Times*. November 21: A1.

Freeman, J. M. 1995. *Changing Identities: Vietnamese Americans, 1975-1995*. Boston: Allyn and Bacon.

Frey, W. H. and R. Farley. 1996. Latino, Asian, and Black Segregation in U.S. Metropolitan Areas: Are Multiethnic Metros Different? *Demography* 33 (1): 35-50.

Garreau, J. 1991. *Edge City: Life on the New Frontier*. New York: Anchor Books.

Giuliano, G. and K. A. Small. 1991. Subcenters in the Los Angeles Region. *Regional Science and Urban Economics* 21 (2): 163-182.

Glaeser, E. L. and J. L. Vigdor. 2001. Racial Segregation in the 2000 Census: Promising News. Brookings Institution, Center on Urban and Metropolitan Policy. http://www.brook.edu/es/urban

Gonzalez, A. 2001. Urban (Trans)Formations: Changes in the Meaning and Use of American Indian Identity. In *American Indians and the Urban Experience*, S. Lobo and K. Peters, eds.: 169-185. Walnut Creek, CA: Altamira Press.

Gonzalez, G. G. 1994. *Labor and Community: Mexican Citrus Worker Villages in a Southern California County, 1900-1950.* Urbana and Chicago: University of Illinois Press.

Gordon, P. and H. W. Richardson. 1996. Employment Decentralization in U.S. Metropolitan Areas: Is Los Angeles an Outlier or the Norm? *Environment and Planning A* 28: 1727-1743.

Gordon, P. and H. W. Richardson. 1998. World Cities in North America: Structural Change and Future Challenges. In *Globalization and the World of Large Cities,* F. Lo and Y. Yeung, eds.: 76-108. Tokyo and New York: United Nations Univ. Press.

Gordon, P., H. W. Richardson, and H. L. Wong. 1986. The Distribution of Population and Employment in a Polycentric City: The Case of Los Angeles. *Environment and Planning A* (18): 161-173.

Gottdiener, M. and G. Kephart. 1991. The Multinucleated Metropolitan Region: A Comparative Analysis. In *Postsuburban California: The Transformation of Orange County since World War II,* R. Kling, S. Olin, and M. Poster, eds.: 31-54. Berkeley: University of California Press.

Hamilton, N. and N. S. Chinchilla. 2001. *Seeking Community in a Global City: Guatemalans and Salvadorans in Los Angeles.* Philadelphia: Temple University Press.

Harrison, R. J. and D. H. Weinberg. 1992. Changes in Racial and Ethnic Residential Segregation, 1980-1990. Paper prepared for the American Statistical Association meetings, Boston, MA.

Houston, D., S. McConville, J. Rickles, and P. Ong. 2001a. Census 2000 Fact Sheet: Residential Segregation in California's Metropolitan Statistical Areas. Lewis Center for Regional Policy Studies, UCLA. http://www.sppsr.ucla.edu/lewis/metroamerica/seg1.htm

Houston, D., S. McConville, J. Rickles, and P. Ong. 2001b. Census 2000 Fact Sheet: Residential Segregation in United States Metropolitan Areas. Lewis Center for Regional Policy Studies, UCLA. http://www.sppsr.ucla.edu/lewis/metroamerica/seg1.htm

Hubner, J. 2001. Hispanic Indians Increase in California, Part of New Workforce. *San Jose Mercury News.* August 6.

Hum, T. and M. Zonta. 2000. Residential Patterns of Asian Pacific Americans. In *Transforming Race Relations: The State of Asian Pacific America,* P. Ong, ed.: 191-242. Los Angeles: LEAP Asian Pacific American Public Policy Institute and UCLA Asian American Studies Center.

Johnson, H. P., L. Hill, and M. Heim. 2001. New Trends in Newborns: Fertility Rates and Patterns in California. San Francisco: Public Policy Institute of California. *California Counts* 3 (1): August.

Johnson, T. 2002. A Welcome Home. *Los Angeles Times.* January 31: E1, 3.

Kang, K. C. 2000. Korean Americans Return to District Torn by Riots. *Los Angeles Times.* April 29: A1, 19.

Kang, K. C. and L. Richardson. 2002. We Can't All Get Along Yet. *Los Angeles Times.* April 27. A1, A18-19.

Kelley, D. 1999. As Suburbs Change, They Still Satisfy. *Los Angeles Times.* October 19: A1, 14-15.

Kelley, D. 2001. Search for Community Prompts Move. *Los Angeles Times.* April 8: B15.

Kempen, R. van and A. S. Ozuekren. 1998. Ethnic Segregation in Cities: New Forms and Explanations in a Dynamic World. *Urban Studies* 35 (10): 1631-1656.

Kotkin, J. 2000. *The New Geography: How the Digital Revolution is Reshaping the American Landscape.* New York: Random House.

Krissman, F. 2000. Immigrant Labor Recruitment: U.S. Agribusiness and Undocumented Migration from Mexico. *In Immigration Research for a New Century: Multidisciplinary Perspectives,* N. Foner, R. G. Rumbaut, and S. J. Gold, eds.: 277-300. New York: Russell Sage Foundation.

Letran, V. 2000. Shopping the Neighborhood: Little Saigon. *Los Angeles Times* (Home Edition). November 24: E1.

Li, W. 1998. Anatomy of a New Ethnic Settlement: the Chinese *Ethnoburb* in Los Angeles. *Urban Studies* 35 (3): 479-501.

Li, W. 1999. Building Ethnoburbia: The Emergence and Manifestation of the Chinese *Ethnoburb* in Los Angeles. *Journal of Asian American Studies* 2 (1): 1-28.

Logan. J. R. 2001a. Ethnic Diversity Grows, Neighborhood Integration Is at a Standstill. Lewis Mumford Center for Urban and Regional Research, SUNY Albany. http://www.albany.edu/mumford/census

Logan, J. 2001b. The New Latinos: Who They Are, Where They Are. Report by the Lewis Mumford Center, SUNY Albany. http://www.albany.edu/mumford/census

Logan, J. R., R. D. Alba, and W. Zhang. 2002. Immigrant Enclaves and Ethnic Communities in New York and Los Angeles. *American Sociological Review* 67: 299-322.

López, D. E. and R. C. Stanton-Salazar. 2001. Mexican Americans: A Second Generation at Risk. In *Ethnicities,* R. G. Rumbaut and A. Portes, eds.: 57-90. Berkeley and New York: University of California Press and Russell Sage Foundation.

Loucky, J. 2000. Maya in a Modern Metropolis: Establishing New Lives and Livelihoods in Los Angeles. In *The Maya Diaspora: Guatemalan Roots, New American Lives,* J. Loucky and M. M. Moors, eds.: 214-222. Philadelphia: Temple University Press.

Loucky, J. 2001. Child and Family Well-Being in Settlement Decisions of Guatemalan Maya Women in Los Angeles. In *Negotiating Transnationalism: Selected Papers on Refugees and Immigrants,* 9, M. C. Hopkins and N. Wellmeier, eds.: 182-201. Washington: American Anthropological Association.

Marcuse, P. 1997. The Enclave, the Citadel, and the Ghetto: What Has Changed in the Post-Fordist City. *Urban Affairs Review* 33 (2): 228-264.

Marcuse, P. and R. van Kempen, eds. 2000. *Globalizing Cities: A New Spatial Order?* Oxford: Blackwell Publishers.

Martin, E. 2002. Questionnaire Effects on Reporting of Race and Hispanic Origin: Results of a Replication of the 1990 Short Form in Census 2000. Final Report of the Census 2000 Alternative Questionnaire Experiment. Washington: U.S. Census Bureau.

Massey, D. S. 1985. Ethnic Residential Segregation: A Theoretical and Empirical Review. *Sociology and Social Research* 69: 315-350.

Massey, D. S. and N. A. Denton. 1988. The Dimensions of Residential Segregation. *Social Forces* 67 (2): 281-315.

McConville, S. and P. Ong. 2001. Examining Residential Segregation Patterns. Lewis Center for Regional Policy Studies, UCLA. http://www.sppsr.ucla.edu/lewis/metroamerica/seg1.htm

Moore, J. W. and F. G. Mittelbach. 1966. *Residential Segregation in the Urban Southwest.* Mexican American Study Project. UCLA Graduate School of Business Administration.

Myers, D. 1999a. Demographic Dynamism and Metropolitan Change: Comparing Los Angeles, New York, Chicago, and Washington, DC. *Housing Policy Debate* 10 (4): 919-954.

Myers, D. 1999b. Upward Mobility in Space and Time: Lessons from Immigration. In *America's Demographic Tapestry: Baseline for the New Millennium,* J. W. Hughes and J. J. Seneca, eds.: 135-157. New Brunswick, NJ: Rutgers University Press.

Myers, D. 2002. Demographic and Housing Transitions in South Central Los Angeles, 1990-2000. Special Report, Population Dynamics Research Group, University of Southern California. http://www.usc.edu/schools/sppd/research/census2000

Myers, D. and S. W. Lee. 1998. Immigrant Trajectories into Homeownership: A Temporal Analysis of Residential Assimilation. *International Migration Review* 32 (3): 593-625.

Myers, D. and J. Park. 2001. Racially Balanced Cities in Southern California, 1980-2000. Public Research Report No. 2001-05, Race Contours 2000 Study. University of Southern California. http://www.usc.edu/sppd/census2000

Navarro, C. and R. Acuña. 1990. In Search of Community: A Comparative Essay on Mexicans in Los Angeles and San Antonio. In *20th Century Los Angeles: Power, Promotion, and Social Conflict,* N. M. Klein and M. J. Schiesl, eds.: 195-226. Claremont, CA: Regina Books.

O'Connor, A-M. 1999. Learning to Look Past Race. *Los Angeles Times.* August 23: A1, 9.

Oliver, M. L. and T. M. Shapiro. 1995. *Black Wealth/White Wealth.* New York: Routledge.

Park, E. J. W. 2001. Community Divided: Korean American Politics in Post-Civil Unrest Los Angeles. In *Asian and Latino Immigrants in a Restructuring Economy: The Metamorphosis of Southern California,* M. López-Garza and D. R. Diaz, eds.: 273-288. Stanford: Stanford University Press.

Passel, J. S. 1996. The Growing American Indian Population, 1960-1990: Beyond Demography. In *Changing Numbers, Changing Needs: American Indian Demography and Public Health,* G. Sandefur, R. Rindfuss, and B. Cohen, eds.: 79-102. Washington: National Academy Press.

Poulsen, M., J. Forrest, and R. Johnston. 2002. From Modern to Post-modern? Contemporary Ethnic Residential Segregation in Four U.S. Metropolitan Areas. *Cities* 19 (3): 161-172.

Pringle, P. 1999. Sheltered Lives: California Town May Show Whether Enclaves Help Latinos Join Mainstream or Hinder Them. *Dallas Morning News.* September 21.

Quinones, S. 2001. *True Tales from Another Mexico: The Lynch Mob, the Popsicle Kings, Chalino, and the Bronx.* Albuquerque: University of New Mexico Press.

Quinsaat, J. G. 1976. How to Join the Navy and Still Not See the World. In *Letters in Exile: An Introductory Reader on the History of Pilipinos in America*, J. G. Quinsaat, ed.: 96-111. Los Angeles: UCLA Asian American Studies Center.

Reed, D. 1999. *California's Rising Income Inequality: Causes and Concerns*. San Francisco: Public Policy Institute of California.

Reibel, M. 2000. Geographic Variation in Mortgage Discrimination: Evidence from Los Angeles. *Urban Geography* 21 (1): 45-60.

Robinson-Jacobs, K. 2002. Replacing Stores Has Lifted Spirits. *Los Angeles Times*. April 21: C1, C4.

Rodriguez, G. 1996. *The Emerging Latino Middle Class*. Malibu: Institute for Public Policy, Pepperdine University.

Rohrlich, T. 1999. Two Studies Find Racial Bias in Rental Practices. *Los Angeles Times*. September 27: B1, 5.

Saito, L. T. 2001. The Politics of Adaptation and the "Good Immigrant": Japanese Americans and the New Chinese Immigrants. In *Asian and Latino Immigrants in a Restructuring Economy: The Metamorphosis of Southern California*, M. López-Garza and D. R. Diaz, eds.: 332-349. Stanford: Stanford University Press.

Sánchez, G. J. 1993. *Becoming Mexican American: Ethnicity, Culture and Identity in Chicano Los Angeles, 1900-1945*. New York: Oxford University Press.

Scott, J. 2001. Census Said to Misplace Many Prisons and Dorms. *New York Times*. November 28.

Shulman, R. 2001. Many Filipino Immigrants Are Dropping Anchor in Oxnard. *Los Angeles Times*, August 6: B6.

Soja, E. W. 2000. *Postmetropolis: Critical Studies of Cities and Regions*. Oxford: Blackwell Publishers.

Soja, E., R. Morales, and G. Wolff. 1989. Urban Restructuring: An Analysis of Social and Spatial Change in Los Angeles. In *Atop the Urban Hierarchy*, R. A. Beauregard, ed.: 87-122. Totowa, NJ: Rowman & Littlefield. Revised from the 1983 version published in *Economic Geography* 59 (2): 195-230.

Stein, K. and M. Libby. 2001. *Stolen Wealth: Inequities in California's Subprime Mortgage Market*. San Francisco: California Reinvestment Committee.

Suro, R. 2002. Counting the "Other Hispanics": How Many Colombians, Dominicans, Ecuadorians, Guatemalans and Salvadorans Are There in the United States? Pew Hispanic Center, Washington, DC. http://www.pewhispanic.org/site/docs/pdf/other_hispanics.pdf

Triem, J. P. 1985. *Ventura County: Land of Good Fortune*. Chatsworth and Ventura, CA: Windsor Publications and the Ventura County Historical Society.

U.S. Bureau of the Census. 1963. *Census of Population: 1960. Characteristics of the Population, California*. Washington: U.S. Government Printing Office.

U.S. Census Bureau. 1992. *U.S. Census of Housing, 1990: General Housing Characteristics, California*. CH-1-6.

U.S. Census Bureau. 1993a. *U.S. Census of Population, 1990: General Population Characteristics, California*. CP-1-6.

U.S. Census Bureau. 1993b. *U.S. Census of Population and Housing, 1990: Population and Housing Characteristics for Census Tracts and Block Numbering Areas, Los Angeles-Long Beach PMSA*. CPH-3-215B.

U.S. Census Bureau. 1993c. *U.S. Census of Population, 1990. Social and Economic Characteristics, California*. CP-2-6.

U.S. Census Bureau. 1993d. *U.S. Census of Population, 1990. Social and Economic Characteristics, Metropolitan Areas*. CP-2-1B.

U.S. Census Bureau. 1996. *American Housing Survey for the Riverside-San Bernardino-Ontario Metropolitan Area in 1994*. Current Housing Reports, H170/94-37. http://www.census.gov/hhes/www/housing/ahs/metropolitandata.html

U.S. Census Bureau. 2001a. *American Housing Survey for the Los Angeles-Long Beach Metropolitan Area, 1999*. Current Housing Reports, H170/99-7. http://www.census.gov/hhes/www/housing/ahs/metropolitandata.html

U.S. Census Bureau. 2001b. Overview of Race and Hispanic Origin. Census 2000 Brief. http://www.census.gov

U.S. Census Bureau. 2001c. Population by Race, including All Specific Combinations of Two Races, for California: 2000. http://www.census.gov

U.S. Census Bureau. 2001d. Profile of the Foreign-Born Population in the United States: 2000. Current Population Report, P23-206, and Detailed Tables (PPL-145), Table 5-2D. http://www.census.gov/population/www.socdemo/foreign/ppl-143.html

U.S. Census Bureau. 2001e. Report of the Executive Steering Committee for Accuracy and Coverage Evaluation Policy on Adjustment for Non-Redistricting Uses. http://www.census.gov

U.S. Census Bureau. 2001f. The Two or More Races Population: 2000. Census 2000 Brief. http://www.census.gov

U.S. Census Bureau. 2001g. Undercount Rate Ranking of Counties with Populations Over 500,000. http://www.census.gov/dmd/www/rates.html

U.S. Census Bureau. 2002a. Census 2000 Summary File 2 (SF2). Tenure, Occupied Housing Units. http://factfinder.census.gov/

U.S. Census Bureau. 2002b. Census 2000 Summary File 1 (SF1). Race: Detailed Tables. http://factfinder.census.gov/

U.S. Census Bureau 2002c. Profile of Selected Characteristics: 2000. Los Angeles-Riverside-Orange County CMSA. http://censtats.census.gov/data/CA/390064472.pdf

U.S. Office of Management and Budget. 2000. Provisional Guidance on the Implementation of the 1997 Standards for Federal Data on Race and Ethnicity. Executive Office of the President, December 15. http://www.whitehouse.gov/omb/inforeg/statpol.html

Waldinger, R., ed. 2001. *Strangers at the Gates: New Immigrants in Urban America*. Berkeley: University of California Press.

Wedner, D. 2001. White-Latino Lending Gap Grew, Study Says. *Los Angeles Times*. January 31: C1, 4.

Weibel-Orlando, J. 1999. *Indian Country, L.A.: Maintaining Ethnic Community in Complex Society*. 2d ed. Urbana: University of Illinois Press.

White, M. J. 1986. Segregation and Diversity Measures in Population Distribution. *Population Index* 52 (2): 198-221.

White, P. 2001. California Indians and their Reservations: An Online Dictionary. San Diego State University Library. http://libweb.sdsu.edu/sub_libs/pwhite/calind.html

Wilson, F. D. and R. B. Hammer. 2001. Ethnic Residential Segregation and Its Consequences. In *Urban Inequality: Evidence from Four Cities*, A. O'Connor, C. Tilly, and L. D. Bobo, eds.: 272-303. New York: Russell Sage Foundation.

Yi, D. 2001. Blacks Cherish Community as Population Groups Shift. *Los Angeles Times*. June 11: B4.

Yinger, J. 1995. *Closed Doors, Opportunities Lost: The Continued Costs of Housing Discrimination*. New York: Russell Sage Foundation.

Zelinsky, W. and B. A. Lee. 1998. Heterolocalism: An Alternative Model of the Sociospatial Behavior of Immigrant Ethnic Communities. *International Journal of Population Geography* 4 (4): 281-298.

Zierer, C. M. 1934. San Fernando—A Type of Southern California Town. *Annals of the Association of American Geographers* 24 (1): 1-28.